"Footsteps Through My Mind"

Book I

Benn Wasson

i

DEDICATION

Many years ago, my granddaughter sat down in my office and said, "Papa, I do hope you live long enough to tell my children the bedtime stories you told me, that I remember to this day!"

Well Court, ten years ago, you presented me with a blue eyed, blond haired great granddaughter that I immediately fell in love with and I have done my very best to fulfill your wish. The bedtime stories I told you have been often repeated; plus, new ones made up on the spot when demands were made for just one more bedtime story. The one with the princess who had lost her leg and met the magical frog who's kiss sprouted a brand new one, went over pretty well.

Now with sand in my hourglass running low, you have presented me with a second blue eyed, blond haired great granddaughter whom I once again have fallen immediately in love with.

What am I to do now with the sand in that pesky hourglass continuing to decline? Turn it over and start anew, of course! Problem solved. The stories go on!

TABLE OF CONTENTS

ACKNOWLEDGEMENT

A special tip of the hat to a longtime friend and esteemed editor Bob Moracezki for his advice and consultation. "Old friends are always the best kind!"

Thank you, Bob!

Immense gratitude to the Canadian, French speaking, talented world traveling business lady, Danielle Lavallee Wasson, for the final editorial and publishing process. Luckily, she happens to also be my daughter-in-law.

Thanks to my wife Betty for a million or more things. To my grandchildren and great grandchildren, much in this book is based on actual happenings, vague memories of possible events, a little fiction and stories told to me by my parents and grandparents. Up to you to figure out which is which!

PROLOGUE

It was misting a light rain. Mourners, umbrellas lifted, were hurriedly saying their goodbyes and hurrying off to their cars. Only the two Salem Cemetery grave diggers, with long handled shovels in hand, were left standing by the coffin. Their silhouette, outlined against the dark gray sky, only made the grim finality of the moment more intense. One went to the back of his pickup, pulled out a long green tarp, and draped it over her coffin. Both then returned to the truck, hopeful of waiting out the rain.

Driving down the sloping cemetery road towards the pavement, flicking windshield wipers seemed to be wiping away the years of her life and memories together as mother and child. She was only forty-seven.

Reaching the hard road, he stopped and looked back at his Mom's coffin for one last time. It was brown with bronze colored handles. A strong wind came up and lifted the corner of the green tarp nearest to him, three times, in a waving motion, as if she was trying to wave him a last goodbye. A vision so moving, it has never left him!

Upon arriving home that evening, he watched television with his wife and children. A rerun film came on showing a young man and his small son walking on the beach in Cape Cod, leaving their footprints in the sand. The image lingered with him throughout the night. The next day, driving to the neighboring town to buy school clothes for their children, he asked his wife to write the word "footsteps" on a small piece of paper and put in the car's glove box.

After they returned home that evening, and his wife and children had gone to bed, he went to the car and removed the piece of paper with the word "footsteps" written on it, from the glove box. Picking up a yellow pad and his guitar, Benn Wasson sat down at the kitchen table, placed the word "footsteps" before him, and just before midnight, completed writing the song "Footsteps Through My Mind."

One of the more touching songs written by a grieving son over the loss of his mother. Played nationwide then, and still being streamed globally, forty years later!

HISTORICAL INTRODUCTION

The heat wave in the summer of 1936 was the widest spread and destructive drought to occur in the Americas in centuries. The hottest ever recorded in the history of the state of Missouri, with 44 days of temperature over 100 degrees. Farmers' crops were destroyed, causing many deaths. It was before the general availability of electricity to any degree, especially among rural residents. Air conditioning and electric fans were regarded as a luxurious novelty, enjoyed by a scant few!

THE SUMMER OF 1936

It was July 15, 1936. Alfus and his wife Mary were tenant farmers on the Missouri plains. Mary was expecting a baby in September.

Corn leaves in the field were curling and dying on the stalk, right in front of his eyes. It was surreal. He had never seen anything like this. The temperature was 118 degrees. It had never been this hot and dry in the history of Missouri. Now, at the most critical time of his life, disaster had struck. Fighting back tears of disappointment as he realized there would be no harvest. No joy of sharing with his wife Mary, and their coming new baby the bountiful harvest for which he had worked so long and hard. His crop was lost. He had invested all his energy and all they had in this crop. They were penniless!

Alfus (Alf) was a promising young farmer. His grandfather, William (Pa) Smith, had replaced his own father as mentor and teacher. William, a righteous man, stepped in, gave them a safe home, and taught Alfus well.

At ten, Alf could plant a row of corn as straight as any farmer in Ralls County. He could cultivate rows so clean, there was scarce a weed to be found. Everyone said he showed a good aptitude for farming. This year, with 44 days of heat over 100, and no rain, nothing could stand up to the merciless onslaught of the drought and heat. He had to give up his farm and the way of life he loved and find some way to feed his family!

SEPTEMBER

It had been a little less than two months since the peak of the July 15th heat wave. Alf had hired on to a timber cutting crew to earn enough money, so they could have food. Railroads were laying rail at a furious pace, needing crossties by the thousands. The intense heat and backbreaking work had nearly killed him the first few days. He could barely eat the meager evening meal his young pregnant wife had prepared for him. However, in time, his stamina increased, and his muscles began to harden. The axe he swung seemed not quite so heavy, and then became light as a feather. Carrying the logs he had felled on his shoulders, strengthened his back and he physically became one of the strongest men in Ralls County.

It is often said that power tends to corrupt and exercising power over the weak is no proof of strength. In Alf's case, his power was purely physical.

IN WAITING

It was September 9th and Mary's time had come! Alf was nervous, scared! He was not the kind of man who scared easily. Just under six feet, broad shoulders, steel blue gray eyes, and a face that revealed he meant to take care of any problem at hand. However, he couldn't handle this problem. He'd heard of women dying at childbirth. It would be the end of his world if he lost Mary!

Mary was moaning softly in the bedroom. It hurt him to hear her in such pain. He stepped out into the cornfield while waiting for midwife Molly Sparrow and Dr. Brown to arrive. He felt more at peace out there. The feel and smell of fall was in the air. Reaching down, he picked up a dried clod of soil and crushed it in his hand. Watching the dust slip between his fingers, he dreamed that someday he would return to tilling the soil, watching his crops and family grow. The dust from his hand gently blew away in the evening breeze. His dreams, sadly, blew away as well.

A red winged blackbird flew up and landed on one of his dried corn stalks that stood in his field. The bird pulled at one of the last kernels of corn from the single dried ear. Two turtledoves, which had been dusting themselves in the loose dirt between rows, scurried over beneath the black bird in the hopeful event a kernel might fall their way. Food for all of gods' creatures was scarce.

Alf's tree cutting work earned enough money for bacon, dried beans, sugar, flour, and an occasional half-pound of candied lemon drops. Mary so dearly loved them. She had craved lemon drops the last two months of her pregnancy. Taking only one per day from the small brown paper sack, she nursed it slowly to make it last as long as possible. To supplement meat for the table, Alf set a twenty-hook trotline just ahead of the riffle on Spencer Creek. The same spot his childhood friend, Dooney, had found his father floating after a night of heavy drinking. He walked to the line each night after work and removed fish that were caught and baited the hooks again for the next day. They had enough food and protein to make a healthy meal for Mary. Providing for one's family had been ingrained in Alf by his rock-solid grandfather William. Alf was a good provider.

The red winged blackbird swallowed the kernel of corn it had successfully pried loose from the dried ear of corn and took flight. The two disappointed turtledoves dusting themselves below, flew off to more promising grounds.

Midwife, Molly Sparrow, arrived just after six p.m. Relieved, Alf thanked her and winced as he once again heard Mary's low moans, while Molly hurried into the bedroom.

MARY

Mary was regarded as one of the prettiest girls in Ralls County. Soft spoken, gentle by nature. Deep blue eyes, near perfect figure, and porcelain white complexion, even though she was a quarter Cherokee from her father's side. Alfus courted her while he was still farming at home. His mother had lived with her father, Pa Smith for two years before marrying a fine man, who believed that work from dawn to dusk was the best way to raise a boy. On Saturday evenings, after feeding the livestock, Alfus would bathe in the nearby creek, saddle up his horse Buck, and ride as fast as he could for the cabin on the hill, where Mary lived. He loved her madly and was jealous as thunder of any man who looked her way.

The small bridge that crossed the creek just below her home was made of fresh laid wooden planks. Mary could hear the hoofs of horses that crossed from her front porch. Alf always had his horse Buck in a dead run when he came to the bridge, riding as fast as he could to hurry up and see Mary. She could tell by the sound of the hoofs when they hit the bridge if it was Alfus, and how long she had to comb her hair and freshen up before her future husband would arrive at her door.

They had been married two years before the baby was due. Mary's grandmother, Gemimia, partly of Cherokee blood, was coming. She smoked a pipe, sat in a straight back chair, and when she heard Mary was with child and her time had come, declared it was time for her to visit her granddaughter.

Alf, hearing Gemimia was on her way, placed a straight back chair by Mary's bed where she was resting. Knowing Gemimia smoked a pipe, he placed a newly purchased red can of Prince Albert tobacco and a small ash pan next to the chair, should she empty her pipe, and need to spit.

The Cherokees were friendly people and had their own ways. However, they took a dim view of anyone who was a dog thief, especially a prized hunting dog. Several known dog thieves from the county had disappeared and were reported to have suddenly moved away to California, never to be heard from again. Of course, California was far away, and poor people from a long way off, didn't have the money to call long distance, or write much in those days. Alfus treated that side of the family with considerable respect.

SILENCE

Mary's eyes were full of fright as Gemimia walked in. "Grandmother, so many girls my age are dying having babies, do you think I'll die?"

"Not likely," she said. "Alfus said he would call a doctor when your time comes and Molly Sparrow will be the midwife, and Molly knows a lot about delivering babies. You'll be fine."

"What about the pain? Will it get worse?" Asked Mary with worry.

"It's always hard when a woman gives birth. There's no easy way to die or have a baby, but the joy of being a mother is always worth the pain," reassured Gemimia.

"I've brought you something," Gemimia said.

"What is it?"

"It's a birthing stick. I made it for you myself. Whittled it out of yellow pine. Pine's a sturdy wood, but not so hard as to break your teeth like walnut."

"Break my teeth?" asked Mary with concern.

The birthing stick was eighteen inches long, with a hand carved grip on each end, smoothly rounded in the center. Many white doctors were amazed when they started delivering babies for Indian women. They didn't scream! Molly Sparrow, in her thirty years as midwife, had helped deliver hundreds of babies, knew all about that.

"White women scream and yell, black women loudly curse their husbands sometimes for getting them in that condition. Mexican women go "yiyiyi", but Indian women didn't do that! They moan, but never yell!" Gemimia went on to explain.

"Why grandmother?"

"Long ago Tribes of all nations fought one another for choice hunting grounds. Then the white man came, driving us from our land. When under attack and hiding from one's enemy, white or Indian, silence can save the life of the entire tribe. If it comes an Indian woman's time, she is expected to not shame herself, or endanger her tribe, by any of that yelling nonsense. When the pain comes, just bite down on the middle part of your birthing stick, it will help ease the pain. Squeeze with both hands on the ends of the stick as hard as you can, it helps push the baby out. Molly Sparrow will come shortly."

With that she knocked the ashes out of her pipe, put the can of Prince Albert in her traveling pouch for further use, and said to Mary:

"Indian tribes have long referred to us Cherokee as the beautiful people. We have never lowered ourselves to do some of the things other tribes have done. Although you're as white as a spring flower, there's a part of you that's Cherokee. Never forget who you are! Have courage! You'll have a loving baby! And don't yell!"

After grandmother had left, Mary relaxed and picked up the birthing stick. Her name was carved in the middle, how loving of grandmother to make this for me she thought. Then the pains came, she placed the stick between her teeth, bit down, and moaned softly. Molly Sparrow walked into the bedroom and a sense of relief crossed Mary's pained face.

ALFUS

Alf shook loose tobacco from his small bag of Bull Durham onto the cigarette paper in his left hand. An owl was hooting in the nearby sycamore tree. He was a Bull Durham man. Left-handed he deftly rolled the paper and tobacco into a cigarette form, ran his tongue for sealant along the paper length, and lit the match. Forming a habit that later filled his life with the deepest regret.

Mary, heavy with child and feeling as big as a barn, had washed two extra bed sheets, scrubbed them white as snow, and placed them on the nightstand next to her bed. She was told to expect bleeding, she didn't know how much, two should be plenty she guessed.

Alf asked midwife Molly Sparrow if she had called Doctor Brown and notified him that Mary's time had come. She said she had called him.

"Doctor Brown has already closed his office and will leave just as soon as he goes home for a bite to eat with his wife."

"Did you tell him which farm mine was?"

"Yes Alfus, he knows. He's delivered babies around here before."

Alf nervously went into the bedroom to hold Mary's hand. She was biting on a stick.

"Molly's here now, and Doctor Brown will be here soon. I love you."

"I know," she answered, smiling weakly.

He noticed Indian carvings on the stick and figured out where it came from. Mary bit down again and uttered a low moan. Alfus hurried back out to the cornfield.

Dr. Brown arrived shortly after seven. His four-door Chevy was painted a bright red. The good doctor wishing to express a little individuality, ordered himself a special painted bright red General Motors Chevy. It would show up good in daylight traffic and come in handy when he was in a hurry to make a house call, like this evening. Drivers would know the doctor's coming.

He opened the car's back door and took out his well-worn leather bag. He had given it one final reassuring inspection before leaving the office. He looked again. It was the young ladies first child and, in these instances, the unexpected sometimes happen. Stethoscope, tongue blade, light source, tweezers, needle, thread, scalpel and forceps were all in place.

A pale-faced nervous Alfus came out of the small farmhouse just as the doctor fastened his leather bag.

"Thank you for coming doctor," he said and quickly escorted him into the bedroom where Molly Sparrow stood with a concerned look on her face.

"Thank you Alfus," and turning to Molly he asked, "Why the long face?"

"Been in labor for quite a time and not dilating right."

The back door slammed as Alfus hastily retreated to the back porch. He wasn't good at hearing language like that.

There is no such thing as a painless birth. Mary's struggle was catastrophic. It had been seven hours since Dr. Brown's arrival, and she was barely dilating. She tried as hard as she could, and her moans were pitiful to hear. Alfus couldn't stand it anymore and left the back porch, walking swiftly into the dried-up cornfield. If he kept moving through the dried corn stalks, the sound of rustling dried leaves brushing against his arms covered up the sound of Mary's moans. Nearly falling to his knees with each deep moan, he kept walking up and down one row after the other. The doctor noticed Mary never made a sound other than low moans!

It was two in the morning. Feeling tired and distressed the doctor looked at Molly Sparrow, and said, "She's already torn. We'll have to cut her more and use forceps. She simply cannot dilate enough to get the baby out of the birth canal."

Molly winced and nodded acceptance. Having seen such conditions in her many years as a midwife, she knew the risk, turned and made the necessary preparations.

Stepping outside the bedroom she called to Alfus and asked, "Are there any more clean sheets?"

"Just the ones on the other bed."

"Strip them off and bring them to me!"

Knowing of course the two sheets Mary had folded and placed neatly on top the dresser would not be enough.

Cutting such a sensitive area without pain medication is extremely traumatic. The top of the baby's head could be seen but it could not get through the birth canal. As he prepared for the incision, he could hear her sobbing and moaning. But there was no outcry. Looking tired and worried, Dr. Brown hesitated a moment, turned and saw the midwife's concerned expression and said, "There is no other choice Molly, sterilize and hand me the forceps!" She paused a moment, looking at him with sad eyes, knowing that many babies die or are severely injured for life from this procedure.

"Yes doctor!"

"It's the only way I can save the mother. She is young enough to have other children."

With lowered head Molly sterilized the forceps and handed them over. He had to push the baby's head back into the birth canal a little to make way to slip each side of the forceps into place. He guessed at placing them on the side of each jawbone hoping to miss the eyes and nose. He closed the forceps and could feel the baby's soft head give a little as the forceps sank into its flesh. As gently as possible, pulling a little at a time, the baby's head gradually cleared the birth canal. Bleeding profusely, the young mother slipped into unconsciousness. The two sheets she had so carefully folded and placed on the dresser and the one Alfus had pulled off the spare bed were soon saturated and dripping with her blood. Dr. Brown, glancing at the baby's face, severely torn on both sides from the forceps, said "Put him on the kitchen table Molly. It's a boy, but there's no way he's going to make it. Hurry! We must move fast if we're going to save the mother!"

There was a small red and white-checkered tablecloth Mary had placed diagonally in the middle of her rough-hewn kitchen table. Trying to make it look as pretty as possible for the arrival her new baby. A brown teddy bear had been placed in the center. With dripping baby in hand, Molly snatched the tablecloth off the table, tumbling the teddy bear onto the floor. The baby was struggling to breathe, its face was terribly torn with blood flowing down both sides from where the forceps penetrated. She wrapped it in the red and white tablecloth and placed him hurriedly back on the table. As she was turning to head back to the bedroom, Alfus appeared and grabbed Molly's arm.

"How is Mary? Is the baby all right?"

"It was a very difficult birth Alfus, very difficult. I need to hurry back to help Dr. Brown, we're trying to save Mary."

White faced he said, "Save her?"

"Yes! She had a hard time of it, but he thinks she will make it. She had a baby boy. However, the doctor said the delivery was so damaging to the baby, he is not going to live. I'm sorry Alf!"

"He's going to die. My boy? Where is he?"

"He's there on the kitchen table!"

"What can I do Molly? I can't just let him die."

She paused and looked down at the floor for a for moment, then raised her eyes and said "Margerie Filigree!"

SIDESTEP - MARGERIE FILLIGREE

Margerie Filigree knew things that normal folks didn't know. She didn't act like anyone else either. Folks described her as a strange woman.

"She don't look at ya', she looks right through ya'!"

She only ate wild honey for sweetening. Scientist recently discovered that a steady diet of organic honey tends to turn blue eyes a lighter color. Margerie had pale blue eyes, so I'm guessing it was because she ate a lot of wild honey! Collecting a tub full of honey from wild bees on the coldest days of winter was common in those days. Bees weren't as active in the extreme cold. Margerie, with all her explorations through the woods, would know which hollow trees harbored a hive of bees.

She and husband Jethro Filigree set up house at the edge of the forest that backed up to the top of Sealy Cliff, a precipice of grey rock that dropped three hundred feet straight down into the deep waters of Spencer Creek. Strange place to live, but she liked it quiet, and they loved one another and that's all that mattered. They had one boy named Dooney. Nobody in his or her right mind ever fooled around with Mrs. Filigree. She was so unusual; kids wouldn't go near their house on Halloween.

One of her many unusual habits was prowling the woods at night, looking for herbs and flowers that only bloomed in the light of the moon. "Rile her up and she might throw ya' off Sealy Cliff," is what they said. Whether she ever did, or would, was of course a topic grown folks held in doubt. Nevertheless, it made a good story and got kids home early on Halloween nights.

Her late husband Jethro had a drinking problem, but for all his faults, she loved every hair on his head, and he loved her. He petted her all the time and called her sweet baby girl. He would pick wildflowers and put them on the table at suppertime and tell her she was the prettiest cook in the whole wide world. Jethro loved to dance. Often, when he came home late at night from drinking, he would turn on the radio and sweet talk Margerie into getting up out of bed for a little dance in the kitchen. She pretended to be mad but really wasn't all that mad. Dooney often heard soft music playing in the kitchen late at night. Jethro would hold her tight and call her sweet baby girl and later Dooney would see them kissing and dancing and then going off to bed. Everything then seemed to be about right in their household.

Margerie usually left the kitchen lamp on whenever Jethro stayed out late. This night, she was tired, had been canning tomatoes all day, and fell asleep before thinking to light the lamp. Jethro's buddies dropped a heavily imbibed Jethro off in front of his home and drove off loudly singing drinking songs. There was no usual light to guide Jethro to his door. The pitch-black night and the drinks he had consumed left him confused on which way to go. He couldn't find the house! People, who get lost, when there is no light to guide them, tend to walk in circles; often coming back to the place they started, and repeat this over and over.

Jethro, although drunken, realized his mistake after a few round trips, and widened his circle.

Instinctively reaching out a searching hand in the dark, brings on emotions lying somewhere between hope and faith. Jethro's outstretched left arm reached into the night as far as possible, each trip, hoping to feel the familiar handle of his back door, unwilling to let go of the half full bottle of liquor in his right.

While Margerie lay in peaceful sleep in their warm bed, Jethro's, outstretched left hand, searching for the handle and safety of his back door, found only black emptiness as his circle swung a little too wide, and he stepped off the cliff edge of Sealy Hill into eternity.

The next morning Margerie woke with a start. Something didn't feel right, reaching over and feeling a cold sheet where Jethro should have been, she knew what that something was. He didn't come home last night! Rushing to put on her clothes, thinking it better to let Dooney sleep, she put on her jacket and started for town.

She didn't know how to drive their car, so she walked the four miles as quickly as she could, asking neighbors along the way if anybody had seen Jethro. No one had. She inspected the haystacks, going and coming, to see if he might have slept in one of those. He'd done that a couple times. But not last night! Upon returning home, a heavy uneasy feeling crept over her. She decided to make her way down Sealy Cliff just to take a look. Halfway down she saw Jethro's cap hanging from a tree branch. Suddenly it felt like a horse had kicked her in the middle of her stomach, sucking the breath out of her. Sometimes you pretend you don't know the answer to an unpleasant something that's about to happen, when deep down inside, you already know.

Margerie found Jethro floating; face down, at the riffle in the bend of Spencer Creek. The deep-water current had carried him down the creek to the riffle where the water gets shallow. A partially subdued tree stump had caught his shirtsleeve, which kept him from floating down further. Using all her strength and resolve, she pulled him out, and partly lifted and partly dragged Jethro's body back up to the top. He was hers, no preacher or anybody was needed or called. She would take care of her own.

Margerie laid him out on their kitchen table, talking to him as if he could hear every word she was saying. Dooney had got up and looked on in a state of confusion. She combed his hair, took off his wet clothes, put on his white dress shirt and new bib overhauls he had never worn. Even ironed out the crease where the pants legs were folded. She and Dooney then dug the grave, under the big maple tree, next to the house. Tears rolled down her face and fell on the wooden handle of the shovel as she was digging.

"Is Dada dead Momma?"

"Yes," she answered sadly. "He's not just asleep, or drunk, he's dead! We'll put him to rest right here where he'll be close to us."

She dug the grave a little shallow, as he had always loved to hear it rain. Their bedroom had a galvanized tin roof, and they would often lie there together and talk late at night. Their bedroom was only ten feet or so away from his grave. The pitter, patter of raindrops, on their roof had often blessed them to sleep. Maybe somehow, he would be able to know it was raining, and hear the raindrops on the roof.

Throwing the first shovel of dirt in his face was the hardest thing she would ever do. She covered up his bare feet first, and then slowly covered up his legs and torso until she came to his face. She just couldn't do that for a while. Sitting down on the ground to rest and compose herself, she thought they might have a little talk first before they said that final goodbye. She told him how sorry she was for not remembering to turn on the kitchen light before going to sleep. There were so many tomatoes in the garden, she had to do something with them, or they would go to waste.

"I canned thirty-two quarts. I got so tired sweetheart," she said. "I just plumb got too tired. Why didn't you holler out if you couldn't find the door? I would have got right up! Why did you have to drink so much?" She stood up then, leaned down and kissed his face softly, saying, "I will always love you Jethro, my sweet boy, nobody else!" After brushing back a lock of hair that had fallen over his forehead, she filled her shovel, and then slowly trickled out, a little at a time, until at last it covered his face. Then digging as fast and furious as possible, she filled in his grave. Margerie Fillagree was now a widow with a broken heart! She never remarried.

The spreading limbs of the big maple tree reached out over Jethro's grave. Maple leaves turn prettiest in the fall. First golden yellow, then red, then brown, and then die and fall to the ground. She and Jethro used to sit together in their lawn chairs on clear nights when the stars were out and look for shooting stars. He told Margerie that if he saw a shooting star first, he would get a wish. If she saw one first, she would get the wish. He wished he could sit out there with her forever.

Although they often argued after he had been drinking, this night a sober Jethro, said to her, "Baby girl, all grown folks fuss with one another about somethin' or the other every now and then, but after this life, when all the fussin's over, I'll be waiting for you there on top of Sealy Hill at that little spot where them pretty wild flowers always grow." He smiled and went on to say, "Maybe then we'll even kiss, and dance a little!"

Margerie, although warmly pleased, would call him a silly old fool and declare, "It's time to go to bed Jethro Fillagree!"

As the years went by, passing travelers would see Margerie sitting underneath the maple tree in the fall, when leaves are their prettiest, alone with an empty lawn chair sitting beside her. She would seem to be talking to someone unseen in the chair. Locals surmised it was Jethro's spirit she was talking to. Her friend, Lucy Dude, was the only one who truly understood. Nobody else cared much, nor mattered.

ALFUS & DOONEY

A lfus handled a team of horses cultivating corn when he was only eight. One of the fields was right across from the Filigree house, and during lunchtime Alfus and Dooney would sometimes play as small boys do. As few people came out her way to visit, Margerie mightily loved having Alfus establish a friendship with her Dooney. He was all she had left of Jethro. Alfus became very much in her favor. He usually brought a biscuit with some meat and a jug of water for lunch. One day, Mrs. Filigree saw him sitting under a tree eating his biscuit and asked if he would like to have lunch with her and Dooney.

"Sure would Ma'am," he answered. Boiled chicken, potatoes from her garden, gravy, and something sweet he couldn't quite make out what it was for dessert.

"Mighty fine chicken Miss Margerie!" he'd said.

She looked down at Alfus with a smile "Mighty glad you like it son."

"Hoot!" muttered Dooney in between bites. As Alfus only had a few minutes to play before he had to hitch up the team, the boys hurried out to play, right after they had eaten the sweet dessert, whatever it was. Noticing some large grey feathers at the corner of the yard Alfus stooped down and picked one up. As he turned it over for a closer inspection Dooney again said, "Hoot!"

"Owl?" inquired Alfus.

Dooney nodded and hit Alfus on the shoulder and said, "Bet you can't catch me!" Dooney was fast and Alfus couldn't catch him. Guess owl does taste a bit like chicken!

Folks wondered if it was true that Margerie Filigree ate owls, hawks, raccoons, snakes and practically every wild critter that lived in the woods, as rumored. Alfus, of course, knew that she did eat owls for a fact, but never contributed to their conversations.

Margerie had a coon dog named Hoover, best in Ralls County. People could see her roaming the hills at night with a lantern, following old Hoover to see where he had a coon treed. While Hoover was on the trail, but hadn't yet treed, she'd take the lantern to look closely on the ground for something she might put in her potions.

She carried a long barreled .22 pistol in a brown pouch to shoot the varmints out of the tall trees. She was so good she could shoot a coon between the eyes at the top of the tallest sycamore tree in the county. Not only did Hoover provide food for their table, baked coon being tasty of course, Margerie skinned them out and stretched their hides to dry over a flat board. Sold them to a fur buyer in New London. Hoover was a good provider.

Often when Alfus was over playing with Dooney, he would notice Margerie putting herbs and roots she had collected from the woods into a boiling iron pot of water. When it cooled down, she poured the yellow liquid into small glass bottles and sold them, mostly to women folks, twenty-five cents apiece. Alfus heard people say the potion would stop bleeding. Several had said she'd put the potion on a piece of rag, rub their wart for a few minutes, and the wart would soon go away. It was also said that she could mutter a few secret words in a sick person's ear, and like as not, they would get better. Seems like they never could quite remember what it was she said. Most people in town supposed she got her strange powers from eating all those owls and hawks and strange things she found growing in the forest. Others even said she got special powers when she swallowed snake hearts, while they were still beating, and could predict the future! Alfus had never seen that, nor would he ask, although there was a good number of snake skins hanging from her garden fence.

Dooney and Alfus remained friends until adulthood. He never mentioned Jethro, except when he woke up sometimes in the middle of the night to soft music. He would crack the kitchen door open and see Margerie sobbing and dancing by herself. "Dancing with Dada," Dooney said. He always quietly closed the door and the next morning, never said anything about it.

On foggy nights, several folks driving down Sealy Hill said they'd swore they saw Jethro Filigree on the road, just before the steep downhill drop off. He seemed to be reaching out with his left hand trying to grab hold of something. Of course, nobody believed them. Country folks make up a lot of things, you know!

Dooney married a Cajun girl he met at a tent revival meeting that was traveling through and spreading the gospel. She was quite a dandy! They moved way off to Louisiana. Good hunting and fishing down there. She said she'd eaten alligator and crawfish and "they wuz real good!" Margerie sorely missed him and always greeted Alfus warmly when he dropped by. He reminded her of course of Dooney. He found out the sweet something Margerie often served for dessert was wild honey and roasted grasshoppers. One wouldn't think so, but they were quite tasty, and he often had two servings.

BATHING IN MOONSHINE

The look from Molly Sparrow was the only clue Alfus needed. Running to the kitchen table, he picked up the checkered tablecloth, it was so light at first, he thought there was nothing in it. Looking again, he could see inside was a tiny baby, his face badly torn and bleeding on both sides. He wasn't sure if he was alive.

"Hold on! Hold on!" he said to his son.

The baby kicked his right leg in reply.

Running to the telephone on the wall he rang two longs and a short. When Margerie picked up he said, "Margerie, this is Alfus, and Mary has had a baby boy and the doctor said he's going to die. His face is all tore up!"

"Is he breathing?"

"Yes, he kicked his right leg just a bit ago."

"Wrap him in a warm blanket and get on the phone right now and call four of your closest neighbors. Tell them to hurry right over to your house and to bring a full cup of homebrewed whiskey. Pour the four cups into a communal pan, say a prayer asking forgiveness for all your wrong doings, then say out good and loud 'Please Jesus, save my son!' Then bathe the child in the communal pan of whiskey."

I never came right out and thanked my Dad, for saving my life. I think he knew it. Nor Margerie Filigree either. I did see her once, through the window, when I was four. She was walking in from the forest to stop by my Granny's house for a visit. A yellow flour sack full of things she'd gathered in the woods was slung over her shoulder. She was a tall upright woman with pale blue eyes that seemed to be looking right through granny. Long straight hair, some strands streaked snow white and some a contrasting dark black, hung down past her shoulders; an overwhelming look for a young buy or for anyone actually!

I could see granny was a bit uncomfortable in her presence. I'd heard grown folks whisper about her mystical powers around the kitchen table. Seeing a woman of such magnitude up close was overpowering. Just too much for a boy of my age to handle. I was afraid if she caught me looking at her out the window, she might turn those pale blue eyes on me and turn me into a frog. At just that moment she abruptly turned and looked right at me. As if she knew I was looking at her. My feet felt like they had suddenly been glued to the floor. To my great relief she turned back to hear what granny was saying to her. Recognizing an opportunity when I saw one, I did what most four-year-old boys back in those days would have done when they faced such a powerful situation...I ran and hid under the bed!

BOBO

I t amazes me that when I ask people when they can recall their first memory, most say five, some even six. Utterly hard for me to believe! I can remember back when I was one. Mom and Dad, when first married, were poor hillbillies. Literally lived in the hills. Our drinking and cooking water were a spring that poured water out of a hillside just below where we lived. Mom had to carry two large buckets of water from the spring each day up to the house. Dad had to go wherever he could find work and would often be gone for some time. Mom was my only source of life! In that situation, I watched her with great interest. I swear I can recall her sitting me by the windowsill, wearing a white smock of some kind, and watching her walk down to the spring, bend down to fill the buckets, then slowly walk back to the house, one bucket in each hand.

When I was a baby, Dad had a dog-named Bobo he liked a lot! They were pals. They would go hunting together, play throwing sticks and the many fun things a man can do with his dog. I had asked him a time or two to tell me about Bobo. He always seemed busy when that name was brought up.

Years later, he finally said "Sit down son and I'll tell you about Bobo!" I was all ears! "He was a German Shepherd! A big one!" I had heard him mention the dog's name to my uncle Fitchum several times, always seemingly in a hushed tone. Why, I could never figure out.

When I was a baby, Dad had to go out to work and be gone for days. Jobs were scarce and he had to take whatever work he could find. His little family had to eat!

During those times, he left Bobo home for Mom and my protection. We never had any trouble with strangers trying to get too close to the house. One winter, times got even harder than usual, and no work could be found. We needed groceries and Dad had no money. He had heard that a man in New London was looking to buy a German Shepherd. He decided to offer up Bobo. He decided to ask for forty dollars for Bobo, which was a lot of money in those days. He figured the man would say that was too much and turn him down. He would find some other way to raise enough money for us to eat. The man didn't turn him down! He brought four ten dollar bills out of a brown paper sack and bought Bobo, right on the spot! It happened so fast, it caught Dad by surprise. He was a tough man, but as he was telling me this story, his face turned solemn and you could sense his regret.

The money helped us through a good bit of the winter. He didn't go back to New London for several months. When he finally had the occasion to go back there, he drove his car by the man's place that bought Bobo, just to see if he could see him from the road. He still missed him! To his surprise, he saw a local fellow walking by the dog buyer's home, and quickly drew back. Bobo had come running out of the doghouse, and lunged at the passerby, only to be stopped by a chain that held him back. It was no ordinary chain. It was a big linked log chain. Dad was shocked! Bobo had never acted like that! He stopped the car and walked up the sidewalk to get a closer look. He couldn't believe it! Bobo's face was torn and covered with scars! One ear had been torn off. He limped on his left front leg. Then Dad understood why the man paid so much money for a German shepherd. He bought Bobo to turn him into a fighting dog. Bobo growled at Dad for a moment, then his one good ear perked up when he recognized Dad and his tail started wagging. He stretched out the chain as far as he could to try and meet Dad. Dad sadly realized the man who now owned him, was a gambler who took Bobo to dog fighting meets to fight other dogs and place bets on who would win. Bobo was still alive! He must have killed a lot of other dogs. It was then Dad realized he had sold Bobo to the worst kind of dog owner ever. Even if he had enough money to buy back Bobo, the mistreatment he had suffered would make him too dangerous for a small child to be around. When he turned and headed back to his car, he heard Bobo whining for him to come and take him home. Dad stayed silent, looking out the window for a long while after saying that. He then got up and walked outside without saying anything else. It still hurt him! I never brought up the subject again.

FIVE

I have no idea why so many events happened to me at the age of five. Most people I know can hardly remember anything that happened to them at that age. For me it was one thing after another. Remembering back, it was quite a childhood adventure. Mostly fun, but not all.

FOUR PIECES OF SILVER

It was terribly hard for a man to find work of any kind in the days of the great depression. Thanks to my Dad's physique, and considerable strength, he could often find employment in far off places where others could not. Mom and I stayed home. There were no houses for miles around, no neighbors to visit, no other kids to play with. Mom and I had to make do. She loved music and played the battery radio every day. I liked the music too and started singing along with the songs playing on the radio. She found I could carry a tune! That was it! She was going to enter me into a singing contest! The monotony of each day was lifted. We listened to the songs being played on the radio, she wrote down the words, and I started learning the songs. The first song was a good toe tapper! It was about a dog, and I could identify with that. "Grab that mule by the tale or else he'll run away", I think was one of the lines. We had fun singing that. It was good to see my Momma smile! She had a hard life! After that was a song that was tougher to memorize, "When the Saints Go Marching In! "Oh, lord, I want to be in that number" was one of the lines. I was five years old! A lot of words to remember at that age.

After, I'm not sure just how long it was, Dad finally came home. He said he was helping build roads and bridges. Mom had me sing the two songs for him first thing. He seemed pleased. Then she mentioned that in two weeks there would be a singing contest at the Salem schoolhouse, and she wanted to enter me. I really didn't know what a contest or schoolhouse was, but if it brought a happy twinkle to Mom's eye, it suited me just fine.

Dad nodded the affirmative, so I sang those two songs twice a day until I had memorized every word. After two weeks, Momma gave me a smile of satisfaction and said, "You're ready!" I still wasn't quite sure of just what I was ready for.

The day of the contest, Momma washed and pressed my good clothes.

Had heated the iron on the cook stove for the pressing part. She then got herself all prettied up, lipstick and all. Momma was a pretty woman. Dad put on his only white shirt, and my Aunt Darlene showed up. She was dressed up too. It was obvious this singing contest thing was going to be a big thing!

After Momma put on my good clothes, she had me sing the two songs for Aunt Darlene. She was a warm friendly woman. She looked at me and said, "So this is the big night?"
Momma said, "Yes! He's ready!"
Dad paused, gave me a serious look, and said, "It's time to go!"
Mom put on my coat and placed a scarf around my neck. "Need to protect your voice," she said. It was cold outside and getting dark.

We piled into the car, Dad and Mom in front, me and Aunt Darlene in back. We had traveled quite a way along the graveled country road when Aunt Darlene exclaimed "A black cat!" I looked up the road and in Dad's car lights sure enough, a black cat was crossing the road right in front of us. "You're sure to lose now!" She exclaimed with a wistful look on her face. I wasn't quite sure why she said that. I didn't learn until later what a black cat crossing your path meant!

The schoolhouse was a big place! First time I had ever been inside one. Cars were parked all over the lot. I'd never seen so many cars in one place. Momma said, "Take my hand," as we walked in the door. It was warm inside, people were everywhere, some spoken to Mom, some to Dad, and then Mom walked me up to the stage. A smiling lady bent down to my eye level and said "Why hello young man. What are you going to sing for us tonight?"

Momma nudged me and I said: "Old Rattler and When the Saints Go Marching' In!"

"Why that's wonderful. All of the other contestants have already sung, let's put you up on stage right now."

Dad lifted me up and said, "Sing good and loud like you do at home for Momma."

There was a lot of smiling faces looking at me, so I smiled back and started singing "Old Rattler." Good and loud! Several of the men whooped and slapped their knees. Everyone seemed to be having a good time. This was fun! I kept right on singing! When I finished "The Saints", the crowd laughed and clapped really loud and I clapped back at them too. Several other kids were marched up to the stage and stood in a line beside me. A man who seemed to be in charge, stood by each kid for a moment while the crowd applauded. When he came to me, the crowd clapped really loud. Suddenly, he lifted my right hand and declared: "The winner!"

The lady who had met Mom and I when we came in handed me four silver dollars. They were big and heavy! I'd never seen coins that big. She then handed me a toy rubber-folding knife. Dad took the silver dollars. I kept the knife.

Everyone was still applauding loudly when I looked at Mom. She had the most beautiful and happy smile on her face I'd ever seen. It was a perfect moment in time. Remembering back, I am so glad I had brought her that pride and joy. She was never as appreciated as she should have been. She was a lovely person, kind through and through. After all these years, I still wonder about the black cat! And will always love you Mom!

MOM

Mom had a grace about her. Whatever she wore, she made sure it was washed clean, and neatly pressed. Made the best of whatever clothes she had. She looked nice in her clothes. She was not a gossip, but highly observant. While others in a room might be rushing to see who could talk first, or the loudest, she quietly, but carefully, observed whomever was speaking and what it was they were trying to communicate.

She once told me, "Son, you can learn a lot more by listening than you can by talking. Learn to be a good listener."

Mom was about five foot five, blue eyed, and of normal weight. She did not curse, had polite table manners, and had more the natural mannerisms of a lady than most. I was her only child. When getting ready for school she made me turn around to see if my clothes were clean and didn't have any holes in them. She would then comb my hair and remind me to pay attention to Mrs. Smith.

I always had the feeling she wished she would have married someone other than my dad. He said he married her because she was so pretty. Long brunette hair and skin porcelain white. He would say, "She's my China doll." By watching him claim his "China doll" like she was his property always made me dislike men who were controlling of their wives. It is a sign of weakness and insecurity, both uncomplimentary traits.

When walking down the street in town, and another man spoke and smiled at her, there would be hell to pay when we got home. It is said that jealousy is a green-eyed monster. That in fact is true! I've seen it up close. It is a destroyer of love and drives those away you're so desperately trying to hold on to, or to keep captive. Some say that if you have a bird in a cage, open the door, and if it stays in the cage, it's your bird. If it flies away, it was never your bird in the first place! Dad often mistreated Mom! She later flew away!

FRISKY, TREE OF THORNS AND THE GLASS SNAKE

The age of five continued to be an eventful year. It led me to Frisky, and the thorn tree! One day, shortly after the singing contest, Dad took my hand and said "Pa's dog Tippy has just had nine pups. He called and said, since you were born on his birthday, you could have the first pick of the litter."

I didn't know what litter meant. It must have something to do with a lot of puppies. Riding in the car's front seat beside Dad was a pretty big deal. First time I had ever ridden there. That was Momma's seat! As we drove up to Pa's farm, I saw his big white-faced bull standing by the barn. Sometimes he bellowed loud scary sounds. I was so afraid of that bull and consequently of all bulls.

Pa Smith was my great grandfather. Salt of the earth! I never saw him slouch in a chair, or anywhere else. He always sat up straight in a chair and walked straight. When going to town, he put on his grey Stetson hat. Looked grand and showed up for church every Sunday morning! I was proud of him. Everyone addressed him as Mr. Smith! They said he had money. He was a good man, upright in everything he did!

When we arrived at his house, he came out to meet us. His wife, my great grandmother, Edith, had died from blood poisoning a year before

I was born. She had stuck a quail bone in her hand that Dad had shot while hunting in a nearby field. Since there were no antibiotics in those days, infection set in. Blood poisoning is a very painful death, and she suffered greatly. My aunt said when Ma was in the hospital, they could hear her two floors down crying out in pain. Pa mourned something pitiful at her funereal. Grandma Edith, his Scottish queen, was the love of his life. He never remarried.

We got out of the car as Pa came out of the house. In his six-foot two frame, he was an impressive figure. To me, he looked like a giant. His steel blue grey eyes looked me over when he walked up and asked, "You alright son?"

Towering over me at the age of five, I meekly said "Yes sir."

He then told Dad and me to follow him and he turned and walked toward the barn. Dad and I followed. The bull was still standing close to the barn. I made sure I walked in between Dad and Pa. Inside the barn was a large basket sitting in the middle of one of the horse stalls. A small grey blanket covered the basket contents. I stood close to Pa and held onto his knee as he bent down and tugged the end of the blanket to reveal the basket contents. It was full of little black puppies with brown faces. I wanted all of them! Their eyes were yet to open, and they wiggled around all over one another. I then felt Dad's hand on my shoulder, and he said, "Son, Pa said you can have any one of those puppies you want. You get the first pick of the litter. Look them over carefully."

I looked from one to the other and my eyes fell on the littlest one. I picked it up. It was a little female. Dad said, "Are you sure you want that one? She's the runt of the bunch!"

"Yep! That's the one I want!"

Dad looked at Pa and said, "Well that's his pick!"

Pa nodded that he understood and said "Pick her up next month. She'll be weaned by then." Pa was a man of few words. He looked down at me and said, "What are you going to name her?"

"Frisky!" I said.

"Good name!" He turned and walked back to the house.

Dad and I got in the car and pulled away. James William Franklin Smith, Pa, always seemed stately to me. To him, life was serious. Promises made were promises to be kept!

When I grew up, I used to go visit him right until a few days before he died. I loved Pa! Seemed like that month lasted forever. Life lessons learned from him guide me to this day.

We moved from the house in the hills into the house Pa built for Grandma Edith, when they were first married, and very much in love. It was a neat little house! Sat on top of a knoll, overlooking the pasture and the barn below. Cows daily grazing kept it as manicured as a golf course. It was perfect!

A sturdy wire fence was built around the house. Served well to keep the cows out of the yard, and me and Frisky in. At first, she could only drink milk. Being the center of my world at that time, I would lie down and put my head right next to her milk pan and watch her lap up every bit. She would then lick me on the nose and run around a little and try to play. I loved her! She started growing and quickly moved up to eating meat and table scraps. Instantly became a kitchen table beggar, jumping around for bites of whatever was being served. I, of course, fed her some of my food under the table.

Most of our hens laid eggs for the kitchen table. Some would start "setting" and stay on their nests and hatch chicks. Mom called the chicks her little dee'dee's. They were as cute as could be. You had to be careful when walking around the yard or you'd step on one and mash it flat. One warm afternoon, I was playing outside with Frisky when I heard one of the old hens over on the pasture side clucking loudly. She was running at a pretty good clip. Seven of her white little chicks were running in a straight line right behind her. I then looked at the last little chick running for all it was worth and right behind it was a snake with its mouth open trying to grab the chick. I shouted, "Snake" at the top of my voice. Momma heard me and came flying out the door with the garden hoe. She opened the yard fence gate and ran out in the pasture to defend the chicks. The snake was so intent on catching the little chick he never saw Momma. She raised the hoe high in the air and brought it down on the snake, then screamed bloody murder!

With the one stroke she cut the snake in two with the hoe. However, instead of there being two pieces, the snake flew apart into five different pieces. It had joints like a puzzle, and you could plainly see where they would fit back together. The pieces individually started wriggling off together, going in the same direction as the snake's head. It was hideous to observe, as you might imagine. No wonder Momma screamed!

As soon as Dad came home, she told him of the horrible snake. He laughed; "It's actually not a snake you know."

"Yes, it was," she said. "Ask your son, he was right there with me!"

"That was a snake!" I said. "It was trying to eat one of the dee'dee's."

"Everyone around here calls them glass snakes! But they're actually a legless lizard."

"Didn't look like no lizard I ever saw," said Momma.

"Me neither," I concurred.

"When I hit that thing with the hoe it split in several pieces. Scariest thing I've ever seen."

Dad explained, "The tail end part of the lizard is jointed so if a predator bites it, the tail parts will drop off and start wriggling. While the predator is concentrating on the wriggling tail, the head and main part of the body wiggles off to live another day. The back parts and tail will grow back in time. Lizards have eyelids and ear holes. Snakes don't have those."

Mom looked at him with doubt, "It's true!" he exclaimed.

"It was an ugly thing," she said.

"Yes, they are. I've killed a few. But you do have to hit them in the head to kill them!"

Mom served dinner, not yet completely convinced!

At the backside of our yard there was a big thorn tree. Its branches extended out several feet in all directions. On the trunk and branches were long needle-sharp thorns. Dad took me by the hand one day and said, "Never play near this thorn tree or underneath it. If you step on one of those thorns, it will hurt you really badly."

"Yes Mom."

Frisky was growing and now could run as fast as me. I would chase her all around our yard, and then she would chase me. On this sunny morning, I was running barefoot through the soft green grass. Frisky and I were having the most fun. When she was chasing me, I forgot and ran barefoot underneath the big thorn tree. I stepped on something dreadfully sharp that hurt real bad and I sat right down to look at my right heel. There was just the end of a thorn sticking out, the rest of the thorn part was inside my heel. I limped into the house and told Mom I had stepped on a thorn. By the time I got inside the rest of the long thorn had gone inside my heel and she couldn't see anything. She looked and said, "You just stepped on something sharp, I don't see any thorn. Maybe you should stay inside the rest of the day."

The next day my heel hurt badly and turned red. "It's that thorn," I said.

She looked at it again and said, "When you came in, I looked and there was nothing there. It must have fallen off on your way in."

"No, it didn't," I stubbornly answered. "It's on the inside!"

"Frisky can stay inside today. Your foot will be better tomorrow."

The next day my foot was swollen twice its size and I said, "Momma, my heel hurts really bad." I couldn't walk on it.

Momma looked worried and called my grandma Bessie, Dad's mom, and asked her to come over. She came a little after lunch, took one look and said "We need to get this child to the doctor before blood poisoning sets in." She knew Dr. Baize in town, called and made an appointment to see him right after Dad came home from work with the car.

All four of us rode into town. Dad carried me up to the doctor's office and sat me down on the doctor's table. The doctor said, "Lay down please." I did. "What's the problem son?"

"I stepped on a thorn." Dad left and went downstairs.

"This looks bad. Something is causing this, and we'll have to lance his foot. No choice."

Momma looked scared, then I got scared.

"We'll chloroform him, and he won't feel anything," explained the Doctor.

He then put a mask over my face, I couldn't breathe, and I fought like mad to get it off. He and Mom tried to put it on and although I was only five, I fought it off again.

Dr. Baize then turned to Grandma and said, "Bessie, I've got to get whatever that is inside his foot out or he's in big trouble. You're going to have to hold him! You hold his arm and leg one side and Mary; you're going to have to hold the other side."

Momma's face was pale. The doctor got out his lance. It looked like a knife to me! Mom and Grandma then each grabbed an arm and a leg, held me down where I couldn't move.

I started screaming, "Daddy!" at the top of my lungs.

I then heard the doctor say, "Hold him perfectly still," and immediately I felt a sharp pain in my right heel.

"Daddy" came out good and loud once again!

When lanced, the infection inside my heal came gushing out and the long thorn with it. He picked up the thorn with his tweezers, held it up and said, "The boy knew what he was talking about! A good thing you called Bessie!"

He bandaged up my foot and Dad came and carried me to the car. He had bought a red balloon in the store while he was waiting. He said, "I'll blow this up for you in the morning!"

When women are talking among themselves, topics not spoken in the presence of grown men come to light. Grandma Bessie, and one of her friends had come in to help Momma cook me a special recovery dinner. They sat me near them in a straight back kitchen chair. Dad had blown up the red balloon and tied it on a string. My morning's entertainment was sitting in the chair and pulling the red balloon up and down. They wouldn't let Frisky in the house; said they were afraid I might get infection in my foot.

They were peeling potatoes for lunch. Grandma was telling her friend Eva and Momma how another woman she knew was not a good potato peeler. "Why she throws away enough potatoes with those thick peels of hers, to make another meal." Grandma always had a kitchen paring knife so sharp; she could peel a potato thin enough where you could read the paper through it. Well, maybe not that thin, but thin! She went on to say, "It's no wonder her poor husband Cleveland, who works as hard as he does, will never have anything!" Frugality was an honored tradition of farmhouse wives.

The next topic they discussed was Elsie Kibble. "She had just graduated from high school. I saw her in church pretty often," Grandma said. "Elsie is a good girl and would make some man a good wife. Church is a good place to meet a man. Church going men have better thoughts and better ways about them. Make better husbands. However, there weren't many eligible young men of her age around there. Olaf Gutzman was eligible, but not much to look at. Eva said she'd heard Olaf had asked to call on Elsie. Olaf had called on other girls in the past with no luck," went on Grandma.

"Why he's over thirty years old," said Momma. "I think Elsie is barely eighteen."

"Doesn't make any difference." "His farm is paid for and he would be a good provider."

I had seen Olaf Gutzman! He was ugly and had a big nose! Elsie was a pretty girl and sat by us in church sometimes. Sometimes she would hold my hand when saying the community prayer. I couldn't imagine her kissing an ugly man like that old Olaf Gutzman. A few weeks after my foot healed, I heard that Olaf had been seeing Elsie, and she was going to marry him. At that early age, I just knew she couldn't love him and was exchanging her beauty and freedom for an ugly man who was a good provider.

When I became a songwriter, years later, I remembered the line "Sounds like you sold your soul to me!" Elsie, I sure hope you did not sell your soul but rather had a loving marriage and a fulfilling life. Because I also learned that the ugliest people can have the most beautiful souls!

THE INEXEPLICABLE

My final recollection of memories at age five you will find difficult to comprehend, but this happened. I've only revealed this occurrence in my later years to close family members, as no one back then had ever heard of something called "Out of body experience!"

It was summertime, shortly after Mom had hit the glass snake (legless lizard) with the garden hoe. Dad had been baling hay, lifting pitchforks of hay onto the front of the hay wagon. It was a hot dusty job. Every so often he would cluck to the horses and they would walk forward a few steps until he said "Whoa!" He would keep adding hay from the front to the back until the entire wagon was full. Then he'd take the hay to the barn, toss it up into the hayloft for protection from the rain. Haylofts in the summer are hot as the dickens. Mom needed groceries from town, so off we went. While Mom and I were at the grocery store, Dad would go to the tavern, for a cold beer. Wanting to get underway she said "Alf, why don't you two go down to the creek and wash up."

In those days water in the creeks ran pure and clean. With no indoor plumbing, in the summertime, men and children often bathed in streams. Dad was covered with dust. Coming out of the house with two towels under his arm, he gave me one then said, "Come on son, let's go to the creek and wash up." It was the same creek and the same spot he used to bathe in six years ago when he was preparing to go for his date with Mom. "Your Momma wants to go to town." No mention was made of his wanting a cold beer.

The water in the creek was running clear, a little more swift than usual. Dad and I took off our clothes and stepped into the stream. It was a little chilly, but you got used to it after a while. Dad went several feet downstream for a little privacy. I stayed behind at the riffle and was much more interested in the multicolored rocks on the bottom than bathing. While running to another spot where I saw some interesting colored rocks, I slipped and fell backwards into the water. I fell on my back and when I tried to get up, I couldn't! The current was too strong and held me down. I could see the clouds and blue sky up above. But I couldn't breathe! I tried harder to get up again. I couldn't! I started to panic! I tried even harder to get up again, I still couldn't! I was drowning! Where was my Dad? I could see the sky through the water, but I couldn't see him. Where was he?

Then suddenly, I could see Dad clearly. His back was turned to me, washing with a bar of soap under his arm. But I was lying under the water. How could that be? Suddenly I got so mad at my Dad! I was lying there drowning and he never even looked around to see where I was. Full panic set in, I was struggling as much as I could, but I just couldn't get up.

Then unexpectedly, I was abruptly up and out of the water, and left standing on my feet. It happened so fast! I thought maybe Dad had come and lifted me up, but he was still downstream washing, and not looking in my direction. Surprised by the feeling of standing up on my feet, I wondered how did this happen?

I really don't know. Could it have come from my own burst of energy arising out of the intense fear of dying, or some other source of energy beyond my field of understanding. Dad never did turn around to look for me that is for sure. If arising from the clutches of the current hadn't happened so forcefully, I would say it was from fear. However, I did see my Dad casually bathing downstream as I was almost drowning. Just how that could happen, I don't understand to this day.

FITCHUM: THE CONTINUING SAGA OF YEAR FIVE

Granny and Papaw Benn lived in a log cabin on top of a hill, in Ralls County. You could see a long way from there. It was made of thick logs, snug and warm in the winter, blessed by a cool breeze most of the summer. Papaw's, Mom and Dad had built it when they were first married and left it to Papaw when they passed on.

My first memory in the cabin on the hill was playing in the house with my new best friend, Frisky. Granny had just opened a jar of canned peaches; flour covered her hands from making the crust for a cobbler, when my uncle Richard walked in. Granny loved Richard! Everybody did! He was tall, movie star handsome, and dazzled everyone.

"Hello Mother. Who is this on the floor?"

Getting a little flour on his light blue shirt from hugging him, she said, "You know who that is! You saw him last Easter. He's your sister's boy, the one who can't pronounce your name."

"Oh yes, he called me Fitchum didn't he?"

I had tried to say Richard back at Easter egg time, but I just couldn't get it out right. I piped up and said. "Hi Fitchum, don't you remember, my name? I'm Bennie and this is my new dog Frisky!"

"Frisky huh! What kind of a dog is that anyway?"

"She's a genuine rat terrier. Her momma is Pa's dog Tippy!"

"Tippy! I've heard about that dog. I hear Tippy is a right smart dog and a good ratter. I think I'll just pick this Frisky thing up and give her a good looking over." He bent down his six-foot frame and scooped her up with one hand and held her up to the light. "Hmmm, not too bad. She is a little scrawny though. I've seen better that's for sure." I was getting kind of upset. Anybody should know Frisky was the best dog in the whole world!

Reaching up I said, "Give her back!"

"Not so fast, I might take a liking to this worthless looking pup."

I reached up for her again and he lifted her a little higher, still not giving her back. I was starting to get really concerned.

"If you want to see a really good dog just look out the kitchen window and take a look at my dog old Boozer. I might even consider trading you old Boozer for this scrawny pup of yours. He's the best hunting dog in this county!"

I rushed to the window. Standing out there was a skinny redbone hound, looking forlorn as could be, and it only had three legs! "It only has three legs!" I exclaimed.

"Got one cut off when I was mowing hay. Don't bother him none though. He can still run fast as the wind."

One of granny's old hens came walking by and Boozer hobbled over to give her a look. "Don't look like he can run much to me," I said.

"He just needs to warm up a little, that's all. Then you'll see he's a number one fast runner." Considerable doubt about Uncle Fitchum and his three-legged dog was starting to creep in. "What time will the cobbler be done Mother?"

"About four or five o'clock this afternoon."

"That's good. Darlene and I will be back to have a bite about then. In the meantime, it looks like Bennie and I have traded dogs. He got the best end of the trade, but that's all right with me."

"Wait!" I cried out. "I don't want that old three-legged dog of yours and give me back my Frisky."

"Too late, a trade's a trade," and carrying Frisky he started walking toward the kitchen door.

Panic and fear set in! I was about to lose my best and only friend. I had to block the exit. Running to the kitchen door as fast as I could, I stretched out my five-year-old arms as wide as I could, and looking six feet up said, "Damn you Fitchum! Don't you take my dog!" That was my first bad word!

Roaring with laughter, he put Frisky down, picked me up, lifting me high in the air said, "Look at him mother! Ain't he a dandy?"

Like everyone else, I grew to love Uncle Fitchum. Whenever he walked into the room things always seemed to get a little brighter. I told Momma that when I grew up, I wanted to be just like Fitchum. He was a neat dresser, had good manners, spoke well, and played the song Four Leaf Clover for me on his fiddle. His fingers flew over the strings like magic! And of course, he had a great sense of humor.

When I became a young adult, we became good friends and used to go hunting together. We communicated so well it was almost like telepathy, not a lot of talk was necessary. A look was enough. There was an easy way between us. Everything just sort of blended in. Can't really explain it, that's just the way it was. I never experienced the ease of communication like that with anyone else again. Blood kin is blood kin, you know! There was something very special about Fitchum!

At my mother's funeral, while standing at her graveside, Fitchum, walked up by my side, leaned over and whispered to me, "Bennie, I'll be next!" That shocked me! He was dressed in a fine brown suit, matching brown hat, and looking grand as always. It seemed impossible. I looked at him and said, "No way Fitchum."

I think possibly the divine might give some people he likes an advanced awareness their earthly time is near an end. A few months later, he had gone to the hospital to see his wife, Aunt Darlene, who had surgery the day before. Walking down the steps beside his grandson-in-law, he said "Donny let me lean against your shoulder for just a minute, I'm feeling kind of tired." Then our beloved Fitchum, died there on the hospital steps of the Booneville Hospital, while his wife was recovering in a room on the second floor. The memory of some people lingers with you always. The warm memory of Fitchum, the uncle I always wanted to grow up and be like, lives with me still.

I didn't learn to the play fiddle, was never as handsome as Fitchum, but I did learn how to play the guitar, sing pretty well, and wrote several songs. One of them "Footsteps Through My Mind", written for Mom shortly after her funeral, was played throughout the nation. I go to church on Sundays and try to be a better person for it. He would have wanted me to be that way.

Thank you for being you Fitchum! You were a comforting example for a boy who at the time needed one!

SIX

The love of a dog is one of life's treasures. It's for the simple reason they love you back. If you've made the biggest mistake ever, your dog will wag his tail, jump up and down and greet you with affection when you come home. You can trust a dog to be like that. People? Well, you can only hope!

Frisky was that kind of friend. I started school a week or so early while I was still five. We had moved to a farmhouse where Dad was going to start farming while continuing his factory job. He had never lost his dream of wanting to farm. Frisky chased mice in the house until they were all gone and then throughout the barn. I followed her on her mouse chasing adventures, and she followed me everywhere I went.

First grade started on September 1st. I was nervous. I was five years old, would be six in eight more days. Momma and Frisky walked me the mile and one quarter across our pasture and down a dusty dirt road to the school. There were eight grades being taught in one little country schoolhouse. A big heating stove in the middle of the room, did a pretty good job of keeping us warm, most of the time. That is, whenever there was enough wood or coal. The big boys sat on one side of the room by themselves, the littlest children were seated in the very front. Momma introduced me to my schoolteacher, then left and told me that she and

Frisky would come back and get me when school was out. They left and there I sat.

Everyone, except one other little boy in the front row, was bigger than me. Then a tall black-haired lady, introducing herself as Mrs. Smith, our teacher, handed me a red sheet of paper and a small cut out picture of a jersey cow. I knew it was a Jersey as we had one just like that at home. She was our milk cow! Dad milked her every day. Baby kittens from the old cat who lived under the barn, would come out with their tiny "meows" begging for milk. Dad would squirt milk from the cow's teats right into their mouths. Dad seemed to enjoy the performance and so did I. Sometimes he let me help him carry the milk in a bucket into the house to Momma.

Mrs. Smith then handed me a round bottle of something white inside. She said, "I want you to paste this cow right in the middle of this red sheet of paper and I'll be back and see how you've done. You do know how to paste don't you?"

I was too embarrassed to say no! So, I said, "Yes!" Which was of course an outright lie! Not having the slightest idea what the white stuff was inside the bottle. I had never seen a bottle paste in my life! I looked around and saw a girl open a similar bottle. There was a brush inside the bottle attached to the bottle cap. She brushed the white stuff on her pink piece of paper. Looked back at me to see if I was looking. Then put the cut out of a doll on the white spot of her pink sheet of paper, tapped it down with her finger, then looked back at me to see if I had observed her performance. I emulated what she had done and waited for Mrs. Smith to come back. I never looked back again at the paste queen. I was too embarrassed.

SIXTH BIRTHDAY

I had survived my first week and a half of school! Momma had walked me to school the first few days and came to get me when the day was over. Then it was Frisky who was waiting for me when school let out. She would leave our house and run a mile and a quarter down the dirt road and be waiting for me. Somehow or the other, she sensed the time of day when school let out. Frisky was a marvelous companion. We had to walk down that dusty dirt road, back to our house, with a big wire fence on the north side. Huge cattle pastured there, and would come right up to the fence, hang their heads over, and menacingly moo and bellow loudly at Frisky and me. Frightening! We thought they might come through the fence and get us! I was still only five, and Frisky only weighed about twenty pounds. We ran home as fast as our feet could carry us!

Some memories you observe early in life etch themselves in your mind and you never forget them. In the second week of my first grade, a young boy named Gary joined Frisky and me on our walk home from school. He lived in a house a half-mile from ours. Luckily the cows weren't hanging their heads over the fence and bellowing at us that day. The afternoon was warm and dry. If you jumped on a little pile of dust, it would puff up around your feet, then blow away. We jumped on every little pile of dust on the road we could find. Grasshoppers jumped up in front of us, make that clicking sound with their feet as they flew away. Frisky had great fun chasing them.

It was September the ninth. As we walked along, I said to Gary "You want to know something?"

"What?" he asked.

"I'm six years old today!"

"You are? Well I'll be!" He stopped and said, "Wait a minute." He put his lunch pail on the ground, opened it, and took out a single banana cookie he was saving to eat on the way home. Handing it to me he said, "Happy birthday Bennie!"

It was hard times for everyone, and all food was scarce. I thanked him and happily munched away at the banana cookie as we walked along. He too was hungry, and he had given me the last thing he had to give. I now wish I had broken it in half and shared it with him. Regret that I didn't. I have remembered his gift of the banana cookie he gave from the heart all these years. I trust he grew up and had a fine life. That banana cookie is one of the two presents received in my lifetime that I remember more than any others!

Most school days went joyfully along, except the one when I had proudly worn my new Captain somebody or the other, plastic goggles to school, that I had retrieved from a cereal box. At recess, one of the boys a year older than me, from a family even poorer than ours, became overcome with jealously and tore my goggles off. Scratched my face up some, knocked me to the ground, then stomped my goggles to pieces. Not having brothers, or sisters for that matter, I didn't know how to fight. I was humiliated, left for home with smashed goggles, and a scratched-up face to show for my day at school. I never told Mrs. Smith.

I also never did forget. A year later, when school started again, I had grown as big as he. Wrestling all summer with some tough cousins, I had learned an art form I found I was good at! On the first day of school, I looked up the goggle smasher and face scratcher and put my newfound art form to work. He was more cordial thereafter.

THE TON OF COAL

My lot soon improved with Mrs. Smith. During singing of class songs, many of the classmates sang out of tune. As they used to say back then, they couldn't carry a tune in a bucket. She noticed I could sing a little. Desperate for some sort of entertainment for the upcoming parent teacher meeting, Mrs. Smith soon, with Moms permission, started keeping me after school to learn to sing songs of her selection for the meeting. I would have much rather gone home and played with Frisky. Mrs. Smith, bless her heart, played a pounding style of piano. I had to sing as loud as I could to get over her decibel level. After practicing for a half hour or so, she would ask if I was hungry. Of course, I always was. Of the numerous after school practices, saltine crackers were the only food item ever offered. The crackers did their normal chemical function of drying out my throat. I would start squeaking on the high notes shortly after crackers. Nevertheless, practice went on and I squeaked and sang until I learned all the words.

At long last, the date for the parent teacher meeting had arrived. Our teacher was of course anxious to put her best foot forward. First on stage were two young girls, sisters, singing a duet. Much tittering between them at first, then they settled down and it went well. Their parents beamed with pride; other parents applauded. Next up was, Herkermer, the son of the most prominent farmer in the area. He usually donated a ton of much needed coal to the school to keep the schoolroom, and Herkermer warm in the winter. The school, operating on a pauper's budget, desperately needed that coal. Herkermer was to recite a poem, and being his father's favored and only son, was given a choice spot, and naturally expected to do well. However, the poet gods seemed not to be present that evening. The long-practiced words, which teacher had reviewed with him so diligently, day after day, seemed to have flown away to some distant land.

From the beginning, the boy, we nicknamed Herk, becoming immediately paralyzed with stage fright, couldn't remember a single word. Eyes, wide with fright, stuttered and stumbled in search of the words he had rehearsed so carefully. Where were they? He couldn't think of a single thing. His face was rapidly becoming as red as pickled beet juice and his eyes searched desperately for teacher to offer lifesaving assistance. With heroic effort, he mercifully at last said something or the other ending with "And he." Hope leaped into our teacher's eyes. Herkermer had spoken! Days and days of schoolhouse warmth was riding on this performance. Stuttering severely, he kept saying, "And he", "And he", "And he".

Sympathetic audience participation took hold. They began leaning forward with each "And he" as if they might help him get it out. However, the "And he" obstacle, stuck in his throat again, seeming to be getting bigger and bigger, ever growing in complexity. Pure mortification was setting in. Mrs. Smith, standing unseen behind the parents, began giving hand signals in an effort to spell key words. Nothing was working. Her exaggerated facial expressions came next. Silently whispering the words, in prayerful hope that her lip movements might return the involuntary fleeing words to the mind of the budding poet. Herk, blankly looked at her as if he had never seen her in his entire life. The ton of coal was about to go up in smoke.

Students, seated on the side, could see Herk, the parents in the audience, as well as Mrs. Smith standing behind the parents. The frantic efforts of Mrs. Smith's hand and facial expressions being performed behind parents, was considerably more entertaining than that of watching the struggling poet. The students turned their entire attention towards her.

SIDESTEP: DROP THE PENCIL

My friend Rickey was the best laugher in school. He sat by me in class. We could look at each other and for no reason whatsoever, start laughing. Can't tell you why we laughed, we just did! He was also famous for inventing the "drop the pencil trick." This hallowed art, only for young boys of small stature, is no longer applicable to the dress fashions of today. However, it was a roaring success back then, and it worked in this way.

Raise your hand to Mrs. Smith and ask if you could come up front and present a written problem to her for review. While she was standing and reviewing the paper, drop your pencil and look up her dress. The rest of we urchins watched Rick perform this feat many times with great success. He had nerves of steel. Admiration and a certain amount of small boy envy spread throughout the school for his creative ingenuity. Sitting next to me, I observed up close his returning to his seat, covering up his head with his coat to conceal hysterical laughter. He invited me to perform the trick. I was most weary, but as is often the case with young boys, the sense of adventure and curiosity, eventually won out. Finally, after receiving his explicit instruction, I nervously raised my hand and approached the front of the class with my paper and pencil. I had added some figures and asked teacher to review them and see if they were correct. While she was standing there reviewing the paper, I "accidently" dropped my pencil and looked up her dress. He was right. It was hilarious! Her bloomers were pink, with many folds, and extending down to just above her knees. They were so heavily built you could have worn them in the Arctic Circle and remained perfectly warm. I wasn't aware any undergarments like that existed, had never seen anything like that in the Sears & Roebuck catalogue that's for sure. I went back to my seat and pulled Rick's coat over my head. He came under with me and we laughed hysterically. Boyhood mischief at its best, or worst?

Soon all boys of small stature had acquired the art of pencil dropping. Rather ashamed now, as she was such a fine person. However, much childhood merriment was created at the time, and I gladly don't think she was ever even slightly aware of being the recipient of the famed pencil drop trick. As I said, she was a fine woman.

BACK TO THE MAIN TON OF COAL STORY

Our teacher's antics, in desperation for Herks success and delivery of the much-needed ton of coal, were becoming hilarious to observe. Herk's face was looking as stricken as if he had been bit by a poisonous snake. His father, the coal buyer, looked troubled and perplexed as well. Rick's head was under his coat again. He was shaking with silent laughter. The rest of us were biting lips and trying not to laugh. Herk, still stuck on "And he", kept repeating "And he" and was desperately looking at Mrs. Smith for help. "And he" what? Her face was distraught.

The Farmer's Almanac had predicted a cold winter and a ton of coal was on the line! To our amazement she started running in place, looking at Herk to see if her antics helped him remember what the "And he" in the poem was about. Mrs. Smith might as well have been insinuating a faraway foreign language. Herk returned another blank look, redder, and more desperate still! Then she hopped a couple of times apparently a running or hopping creature was involved in there somewhere. With that the students, now watching every move she made, had stood all they could stand. They howled in a roaring torrent of laughter. Rick fell out of his chair from laughing so much. The rest of the audience, unable to witness Mrs. Smith's antics going on behind, but knowing something must be incredibly funny, broke into sympathetic laughter as well.

Game to the end, our teacher, ran up to Herk and whispered lifesaving words into the ear of the poet. Recognition set in! He blossomed like a rose on a spring morning after an early rain and finished the poem! The audience, full of parents knowing the same thing could have happened to their child, gave Herk a fine round of applause. His father, hearing the applause, looking somewhat dazed, instantly became a beaming happy father and nodded in friendship to all those seated around him. Herk was his boy!

Suddenly I was on stage, singing away. I remembered all my words. Mrs. Smith, pounding the piano for all she was worth, flashed me a grateful smile when we finished without error. The parents applauded, and with a look of relief, she loudly exclaimed, "Let the pie auction begin!"

THE FLY IN THE PIE!

The performance of the students was merely the warmup act for the school's big parent teacher moneymaker, the pie auction! Every mother, grandmother, aunt or whomever would pull out her best pie recipe, put on her apron and begin baking for the honor of their pie bringing the highest bid at the school auction. Prestige and honor of her household was at stake! The coal and wood supply, necessary for the schoolhouse warmth of the children, was the big expenditure. Pencils, paper, books, and numerous other incidentals also added up. None of us realized it at the time, but Mrs. Smith probably bought many of the items out of her own meager salary. She was a good soul.

Momma's coconut cream pie took second place last year. Her goal was to take first place this year. She had canned a jar of cherries picked fresh from our tree last spring. They sat red and beautiful on the pantry shelf. They would make a wonderful pie! Regardless how much I hinted, even pleaded for a cherry pie, her stance was as immovable as the rock of Gibraltar. No cherry pie for Dad or me! She had a plan.

When I brought home the note from school that the pie auction would be held Friday evening, Momma got up from the kitchen table, opened the door to the pantry, and looked at the cherries for a moment. She rubbed her hand on her chin, and then in deep thought, sat back down. Student entertainment, provided by the singing sisters, poetry reading, and an ending solo would start at six p.m. I was the ending solo. All pies were to be in place and displayed on the long table before entertainment. After student entertainment there would be thirty minutes for rest and visitation, with the pie auction starting promptly thereafter at seven p.m.

Friday morning, Momma slowly and deliberately, took down from the pantry shelf; the world's most beautiful jar of cherries. She carefully placed this red treasure in the middle of the kitchen table, and again put her hand underneath her chin, and stared at it for a moment. Then I heard her say the word, "Lattice!" I thought she said "Lettuce!" I went off to school with Frisky, wondering what lettuce had to do with a cherry pie. That afternoon, I came home to see the kitchen table covered with flour. The pie crust had been rolled thin, cut in strips, and crisscrossed across the top of cherries in the pie.

"That's a lattice decorated pie," she said. The crust was golden brown, enhancing the ripe red cherries showing underneath, creating a colorful gourmet dance.

"That's a pretty pie Momma!"

"Yes, it is," she said, "even if I do say so myself. The real butter we got from Old Jerse (our cow), this morning is in that crust!" You could see she was dressing up the cherry pie to go out for the evening. It indeed looked very grand and was sure to be well received!

By five thirty, just prior to the entertainment, the long table, displayed pies of all kinds and flavors! Namely: apple, cherry, peach, chocolate, butterscotch, pumpkin, gooseberry, blueberry, blackberry, and lemon meringue. Men, who would do the bidding, would slowly peruse by the table, carefully examining each pie. They were hard working farmers who thoroughly enjoyed the taste of a good pie. With money so scarce, they were expected to choose well for their family.

The pies of many colors were beautifully done, that is except one. Mrs. Goodson had baked a lemon meringue pie. I had been in her house occasionally, visiting her son who was near my age. She and her husband had many children. She had recently purchased a new pressure cooker to prepare meals faster for her ever-increasing brood as she did her many other necessary household chores. Not all had gone well, as one could plainly see beans imprinted on her ceiling, indicating the cooker's pressure had got a bit out of hand, blown up, gracing the ceiling with bean evidence. Her hair always seemed to be uncombed, and with all the unwashed children running around in every direction, you could understand why. She seemed continually distraught and exhausted I'm sure. Poor Mrs. Goodson!

When she brought in her lemon meringue pie, one of her many smaller children, running about, pulled hard on her dress, just as she was placing her meringue pie on the long table. Losing her balance, Mrs. Goodson abruptly jerked her hand holding the pie, causing half of the light, fluffy, sugary egg beaten meringue on top, to flip up! Half of the pies bright yellow lemon that had nestled so nicely under the meringue was rakishly exposed for all to see. No way to amend the pie for appearance sake. As light and delicate as the meringue was, she couldn't possibly straighten it out. The yellow part of the lemon pie would just have to remain exposed. Nevertheless, it was a pretty color yellow, and would taste just fine.

Not everything in life comes about as one had wished. Green pastures, whose residents were large cows that mooed loudly at little boys and their dog as they walked to school, surrounded the schoolhouse. They also deposited large numbers of cow pies in the field of which they resided;

grateful flies comfortably dined on said pies throughout the summer. However, summer was in its waning days, fly food was getting scarce, and one fly, in desperate search of nourishment, made it through the front door of the schoolhouse. Apparently, the bright yellow of the lemon pie proved irresistible. After circling two or three times, his chosen place to land and feast was right in the middle of the exposed yellow part of Mrs. Goodson's lemon pie.

Now anyone who knows the slightest bit about art knows that contrasting colors brings attention to the subject at hand. In this case, the subject at hand was the black fly in the middle of Mrs. Goodson's lemon meringue pie. The yellow lemon was very bright and lovely in coloration. The contrasting color of the black fly, and the bright colorful lemon, riveted one's gaze to the spot where it had been sweetly caught. If the fly had eaten all the lemon pie it could hold, then passed away peacefully in a glucose overload, it would have been bad enough. However, the fly, stuck in the sweet embrace of the unrelenting pie, remained very much alive! In its struggle to gain freedom, it had tilted over on its left side putting the left wing out of commission; however, it's right wing, sticking straight up in the air, remained well and operational, rapidly fluttering in a never ending futile attempt to take flight and escape his sweet embrace. The bright beacon of the lighthouse on the coast of Maine couldn't have done a better job of concentrating one's attention to that exact spot, than the fluttering wing of the black fly, stuck in the middle of Mrs. Goodson's lemon pie.

Bidders of the auction were summoned to the pie table. All men, all farmers, with each one knowing full well the dining practice of flies, rose from their seats and headed for the table. Mrs. Smith first lined them up to walk on the right-hand side of the table for viewing purposes. They slowly walked by each pie, taking a careful look. Money was scarce and not to be fiddled away on some no-account pie. The yellow part of Mrs. Goodson's pie, with its captured fluttering prisoner, was on the right side of the table. Farmers, notoriously shrewd buyers, cast a narrow eyed sideways look at Mrs. Goodson's pie as they carefully walked buy. Stoic they were, showing no emotion of any kind. A seasoned Las Vegas poker player couldn't have done a better job of concealing their emotion. Sharing a pie with a fly, of course, would not be an inclination in their nature. Each farmer turned at the end of the table and walked back down the left side so that a full view of each pie on each side could be observed. Momma's cherry pie was on the left side.

The bidding started. Momma's cherry pie, with the lattice crust design, was auctioned off first. It brought a good price. She looked confident. Second to be auctioned was last year's pie winner. This year she had baked a crumb topped, apple pie. Nothing could stand up to the cherry lattice! Momma's carefully thought out lattice designed cherry pie beat hers by three dollars. No one else came close. Momma was now the undisputed champion pie baker of our little schoolhouse community. They auctioned off Mrs. Goodson lemon pie, last.

The auctioneer pretended he didn't notice the fly in the pie and said, "Now, who will bid five dollars for this beautiful lemon pie?"

Hard faced fly swatting farmers moved not a muscle.

"Well then who'll give me a four-dollar bid?" No response. "Well now, surely a bid of three dollars is out there." Still no response!

The crowd was looking uncomfortable.

"Two?" Finally, Mrs. Goodson's husband bid twenty fine cents and got it with no counter offers made.

That was the last pie supper I would ever see auctioned at our tiny school. World War II had started! Neighbors, and friends, and family members went overseas to fight! Yellow stars were on the windows of many sad faced households.

A heavy frost fell upon the little one room country schoolhouse the first week of November. Mrs. Smith noticed grey clouds, riding on an incoming northern breeze, blowing fallen leaves across the schoolyard. Cold weather was coming. Her husband had charitably cut a chord of stove wood for the big heating stove in the middle of the school before he got sick. It was nearly gone, and he hadn't been feeling well enough to cut more. Something had to be done. That afternoon there came a knock on the schoolhouse door. No one ever did that. All the children turned in unison to see who this mysterious stranger might be. The door opened and hallelujah! It was the good farmer, the father of Herkimer the rising poet. He took off his cap when our teacher opened the door. The ton of coal, that lifesaving fuel that protected small children from the winter cold, had arrived. This kind man continued his warmth giving annual tradition by delivering an annual ton of that life supporting commodity, until the little one room country schoolhouse closed for good. Herkermer grew up and did quite well.

SIDESTEP: CAT FAMILY

Towards the end of my first grade of school, my walking home buddy, Gary and I, came across a family of cats. They were obviously near starving. There was a mother cat, a one-eyed father cat, and four kittens. They didn't have much hair and meowed constantly for food. Gary didn't have a thing left from his lunch box from school. I had one slice of bread and tore it into multiple pieces and scattered it around so each cat might get something to eat.

Well that was it. They rushed over to me, walked around my feet so close I practically tripped and fell over them twice before arriving home, meowing all the way. I was hoping Dad would let me keep them. Dad and my visiting cousin were in the barnyard unloading some feed when I walked up.

Dad looked at me and said, "What in the hell are you doing bringing home those mangy cats. Don't you know they have a skin disease?" He turned to my cousin and said, "Go get my rifle." Since I was always a little afraid of Dad, I didn't say anything, but felt most apprehensive. I was afraid he was going to shoot them outright. If he had shot them right there on the spot, it would have been much the better. Instead he and my cousin chased and caught all of them and put them in a large burlap sack. There was much meowing coming from the sack.

He then said to my cousin, "We might as well use them to train these new hunting dogs we need to break in. At least they'll be good for something." I didn't understand what he meant. He went to the kennel and let loose the three hunting dogs and they immediately rushed to the sack, growling and sniffing. They were hunting dogs. Tall, rangy, had long ears, sharp eyes, and anxious for action. He told my cousin to hold the rifle for him and for me to step back out of the way. I still didn't know what was going on. Dad teased the dogs with what he had in the sack, then suddenly, he let loose one of the kittens. With those dogs growling and barking behind him that kitten ran fast as the dickens, real fast, but not fast enough. The hunting dogs caught him. It was a quick ending. Dad let the other three kittens out one at a time with the same screeching result.

Then he let out the mother cat. She put up a little bit of a fight, but they were tall rangy hunting dogs, and she was a cat. Lastly, he let out the big one-eyed tomcat. He was bigger and faster! He outran the dogs to a tall wooden telephone post at the edge of the field and climbed to the top. He had escaped! As I looked at the cat perched on the top of the tall pole, I witnessed one of the oddest things I've ever seen in nature. Never seen anything like it again. The tomcat stood tall, puffed up his chest, and looked down at us with his one good eye in utter disdain. Clearly showing us he had won! He was the victor. He was gloating! Nothing else to call it! It was cat put down and he reveled in his victory! A surreal scene! Tom Cat was the king! We were his lowly tormentors. It's never wise of course to gloat over one's victories. Dad reached his hand out to my cousin for the gun. He raised his rifle, took aim, and shot the cat dead. I had never experienced such a bizarre few moments as this.

I then worked up my courage, stood in front of Dad and said "Why?"

For a moment his blue gray eyes turned to steel, and I thought I might get smacked for a row of stumps. But his face calmed down for a moment and said, "Son, those cats had an infectious disease. If I would have let that tomcat go, he could have infected both wild and tame animals all over this county, and they would have all died a terrible death. We'll bury these cats. I'll wash our dogs with cider vinegar for protection and they will be all right." He turned to go, then stopped a moment, turned back again, looked at me now steely eyed and said "Boy, don't you ever drag home a mess of cats like that again!"

I never did!

BING

Some episodes when you're young remain in your memory regardless of how long ago they happened. One was our dog Bing. He was a pure white dog. Drifted in one day from somewhere, shortly after we had just moved to the farm. No collar, no one came looking for him, so he just settled in. Mom and Dad liked him, so did I, he didn't bother the hunting dogs or Frisky, so he had found a home.

He was basically uneventful. He would go hunting with the other dogs but would never jump right into the hunt. Sort of tag along and watch interestedly while the hunting dogs fought a huge male raccoon. Barked enthusiastically but never offered to help. Trotted into the forest with the rest of the dogs for the hunt and trotted right back out with never a scratch. Respectable observer. Always seemed appreciative of the hunters, and most happy to have gone along. That was o.k. Everyone got along, things were fine, we liked Bing and that was that.

In October, the fall of 1943, a fellow with a truck full of apples stopped in at the farm selling bushel baskets full of ripe red delicacies. They were nice apples! The apple seller's young daughter, blond headed as I recall, riding in the back of the pickup, got out and starting petting Bing. They seemed to get along quite well. Dad asked where his apple orchard was, and he said a little over a hundred miles away. He and Dad talked awhile, and he asked Dad if he was sure he wouldn't buy a bushel of apples. Dad said they were just too high but added "I've noticed your daughter has taken a liking to that white dog. I will trade that dog to you for a bushel of those apples." I looked at Dad in total disbelief! I wanted to speak up, but I knew better. I'd been backhanded and slapped flat a time or two for speaking out of turn, so no use inviting disaster. Disaster comes soon enough without extending an invitation.

The apple man went to the back of his pickup and took out a bushel of apples, and handed them to Dad, who in turn picked up Bing and put him in the back of the pickup alongside the little girl. I stood there stunned as I watched Bing, perched alongside the blond headed little girl, surrounded by baskets of red apples, pull away and out of sight.

Things were no longer fine. A pleasant, congenial, member of our family was gone. Traded away! I wouldn't eat any apples for two days. One morning Mom came out of the kitchen wearing a blue apron and said, "There's no use you just sitting there pouting. Bing's gone and these are good apples! They're good for you!" Handing me an apple she continued, "Take a bite, they taste really good!" They did!

February soon arrived. It was proving to be a cold hard winter. Seems like I could never keep enough coal in the stove to keep the house warm. That was my job. Carrying in buckets of coal and putting it in the stove.

Weekdays, usually about four every afternoon, the mailman came by our farm. Mom, always anxious to see if one of her relatives had written asked me to go out and check the mailbox. I looked into the mailbox it was empty. Glancing to my right I thought I saw a dog coming up the highway. It was limping badly, so I paused for a moment to get a better look. When I did the dog raised his head and saw me. It yelped and hobbled faster in my direction. I thought, "This can't be!" I called aloud "Bing!" He yelped again and tried to run even faster but tripped and fell. He tried to get up but couldn't, he was too weak. I picked him up. He had lost a lot of weight and carried him easily to our storehouse that was sheltered from the cold and wind. He raised his head slightly, looked up at me, and wagged his tail a little in thanks.

Mom had seen me carrying him in. She had a couple old blankets and placed one under him to lay on and another on top to keep him warm. I noticed his footpads were virtually worn out, some were bleeding. Mom brought a pan of warm water, a cloth and some salve. I began washing his feet and put salve on the cut wounds/

"Good God!" my mother said. "This poor thing has found his way back home from all that distance. Over a hundred miles! He'll never leave our home again."

When I had finished, Mom placed a warm pan of milk in front of him and I held up his head so he could drink. He lapped it right up. Upon finishing, he let out a big sigh and laid his head back down. Looking up at me he wagged his tail again in thanks as I walked out the storehouse door. I had missed him!

"I'll be back in the morning Bing!"

Mom tucked him under the warm blankets, and he fell asleep. It had been a long arduous journey.

I went out to look at him again after supper and he was still asleep. The covers were just as Mom had placed them. He was breathing evenly. When Dad came home, he too went out in the store house, looked at Bing laying there sleeping, and said "This the strangest thing I've ever seen." During the night, about two in the morning, Bing made a long mournful howl, then, was quiet. He had suffered much and long.

In the morning, Mom handed me a small pan of warmed meat and said, "Take this to Bing. I hope he's better this morning."

He hadn't moved much so I placed his food just in front of his nose saying, "Get up Bing! Get up old boy, I've brought you something to eat."

He didn't move. I shook him a little, but there was no response. I lifted his front leg and it fell back lifeless. Someway or the other Bing, though struggling and suffering much, made it back from such a long way to where his heart was. We were his family. He had died during the night. The long mournful howl we heard around two o'clock was Bing telling us he had made it home, it's where he wanted to be, it's where he had come to die. His lonesome howl was his way of telling us he was leaving us, and he was sad to go. The memory of it has stayed with me all these years. All of us felt guilty. Especially Dad.

I was so glad I had carried him to the storehouse, and that Mom and I had washed his feet and dressed his wounds. Covering him with blankets to keep him warm and giving him a pan of warm milk, showed him we were glad he was back home, and we cared. Dad dug a grave and gave Bing a proper burial out in the corner of the pasture. As I walked back to the house, I remembered his looking at me last night, just before I closed the door, and wagging his tale in thanks and a last goodbye.

This unique emotion we call love, transcends our species, and can be felt between man's oldest pet and ourselves. They become a loved member of our families. And to this day, I believe that it was not right in any way to trade off a member of our family for a basket of red apples.

Benn Wasson

AGE EIGHT

HARD TEARS

My Dad still had the love of working the soil in his veins. It was part of his childhood. It was a part of who he was. He saved enough money working at the plant to add cattle to his small farming operation. His job at the factory was that of a molder. They had molds of wood, filled with clay, then the mold had to be raised up and down by hand numerous times until the clay had perfectly formed to the mold. Then it was taken to the oven to be baked into a permanent tile. It was hard work. Repeating that procedure many times a day built his arms to where they were big as a man's leg. He bought three calves at a cattle auction to raise and sell for profit when they got bigger. He then went to Pa, his grandfather, and asked if he could buy a heifer. Pa had a herd of purebred Herefords, among the best in the county. Pa didn't believe in giving relatives everything they asked for. He said, "If people work for what they want, they earn respect for themselves along the way and they become stronger." On the other hand, he said, "If you give them everything they want, without their doing anything for it, they never appreciate the gift, or the hard work it took to get it." He gave Dad a fair price, but he had to pay for it. Dad borrowed the money from the bank, and he paid Pa in full. It was one of Pa's prize heifers.

MIDGE

Midge was perfectly formed as cattle go, with a full white face and brown body. He said to Dad, "This is the best heifer in my herd. When she matures breed her to a pure-bred Hereford. If she has a male calf, raise it, sell him, and use that money for your farming operation. If she has a heifer, raise but keep her, breed her back to another pure-bred Hereford bull and when she has a calf, you'll have started building your herd."

One other thing I often heard him say, "Always save a nickel out of each dollar you earn, and you'll never be poor!"

Pa was not only a rock-solid man he also knew how to manage a farm and money.

Winter had passed, and spring rains had arrived. Mom ordered in fifty baby chicks from the hatchery in February, kept them warm in the hen house during the cold months, and it was now warm enough to let them out to roam in the chicken yard. Seeing baby chicks running around is always a welcome sight. Some rooster chicks would quickly grow more than others and become fried chicken for the table. You couldn't just go to the store and get a chicken in those days. If you wanted fried chicken, you had to wait until one of them grew big enough to harvest. Everyone kept an eye out for the biggest young rooster. We hadn't eaten fried chicken for six months.

School was out and it was the summer of 1943. During that night we had a bad storm. Lightening and thunderbolts struck in every direction. Frisky even jumped in bed with me for protection. Not sure if it was for his or mine. The sun came out the next morning to a clear sky. Sometimes when it rains good and hard the earth looks like it had a welcome bath. The sows were rooting around in the ground as pigs normally do.

We had two roosters. One big white rock and one little bantam, crowing like crazy most of the time. They didn't get along and fought almost daily. However, it wasn't the big white rock that started the fights. It was the little bantam! He was an ornery little bird, always looking for a fight and he always lost! Sometimes they would fight half the day. Occasionally the little bantam would get completely knocked out. You would occasionally walk by and see him lying there, and figure he had finally overdone it this time. Instead, the next morning he would be up crowing again as pretty as you please, and ready for another fight. Midge and the other three calves were usually in the barnyard by this time in the morning, bot no sight of them today.

Mom and I glanced at the barnyard every once in the while to see if they had come up to the pond to drink or nibble on some hay that Dad had spread out. Nothing. Then Mom said, "They could have broken through the fence and gone over into the neighboring farms' pasture, all that thunder and lightning probably scared them." Cattle are notorious for getting through or jumping a fence. "Your Dad is usually exhausted when he comes home from work. He sure won't feel like chasing them down and herding them back to our pasture and maybe even have to fix the fence. Maybe you can go with him and help do some of the chasing." She looked out the other window to the neighbor's pasture but did not see them. We were both getting worried.

A little after five, Dad came in from the plant. Pouring himself a glass of iced tea Mom had made, he sat down in his easy chair and started to kick off his shoes.

She said, "No sense pulling off your shoes, the cattle must have got out. We haven't seen them all day."

Dad was a tough man. Mean sometimes, but he did work hard to feed and clothe us. He gave a deep sigh and said to me "Do you want to come with me and maybe help do some of the chasing?"

"Sure."

"Bring a handkerchief with you so they can see when you wave and won't run over you."

I took a big white one that Mom had been ironing in the kitchen and stuffed it in my rear pocket.

As we walked along together, it was comforting to just be with my Dad for a few minutes, all by ourselves. No arguments between he and Mom. I hadn't done anything to deserve a whipping. Everything was clear there. We were just strolling through the pasture together, looking for our cattle. It was as it should be between father and son.

Our wire fence ran straight out from the barn for about a quarter mile, then took a right-angle turn, ran straight for another half mile, then hooked up with our neighbor's fence and then ran on straight for another half mile. Quite a lot of fence! A meadowlark jumped up from beneath my feet and flew away. Startled me! At first, I thought it was a quail and said so to Dad. He laughed and said, "They've fooled me many times like that too."

About then, we reached the fence's right angle and turned for the straight half mile section headed north. Suddenly Dad stopped as if he was frozen in his tracks.

I looked ahead to see where his gaze was riveted. Midge and the three other calves were lying down by the fence. I said, "Look Dad, there they are! They're sleeping"!

Then Dad whispered softly, as if to himself, "Dead! They're all dead!"

I couldn't believe what he had just said! It was unreal. They looked so peaceful, lying there together. Surely, they'd get up any minute now and head back to the barn.

I walked up to Midge and touched her shoulder; it was cold. I turned and said, "Dad! How?"

"Lightening", he said, "Lightening!"

His face was ashen white, and tears were streaming down his face and falling on his blue shirt. I was shocked! I had never seen Dad cry! I had never seen any grown man cry! Anywhere! As I think back, I now know his hopes of building his own herd had died there with Midge, Pa's pride of the herd. He started to wipe his tears with the back of his hand, and I pulled out Moms big white handkerchief from my hip pocket and said,

"Here Dad."

"Thank you, son."

He'd never said that to me before, ever.

"We need to go back to the house and call the dead animal truck to come pick them up and tell your Momma."

Many people do not understand the rudimentary danger of lightening. It doesn't just kill people or animals in the spot where it strikes. It can travel through fence wire long distances and jump off. That's what Dad said happened to Midge and the calves. The lightening had hit our neighbor's fence that was connected to ours a half mile or so away, traveled down the fence to where Midge and the calves were standing, jumped of and electrocuted all of them. It was a long sad walk back to the house.

NARROW ESCAPE, PEANUT BUTTER, APPLES, THE BIG TURTLE, AND GOODBYE TO DAD

They say when it rains, it pours. It sure did for our little family. It was Saturday, Dad was off work, the dead animal truck had come and picked up Midge and the other three dead calves. Things were solemn. I had been outside playing with Frisky. Things were bad, but when I walked in, I wasn't expecting to see Mom sitting at the kitchen table crying. Dad was sitting there next to her, white as a sheet again, like he looked when he saw Midge and the calves lying dead by the fence out in the pasture. Both were holding onto a letter that I had brought in from the mailbox earlier in the afternoon. It was from the government. Dad had been drafted into the Army! He had thirty days to get his affairs in order and report for duty. They were shocked! He was being called to go fight in the war!

As I sat down at the table Dad said to us, "I borrowed money from the bank to buy Midge and the calves. If they hadn't been struck by lightning, I could have sold them and paid off the bank. Now I have to find some way, in thirty days, to pay back the money I owe. I might not come back from the war and I wouldn't want to leave my debt weighing

85

down on you. That's not the memory of me I would want to leave behind."

Gold stars were placed in the windows of families whose boys and men had got killed fighting in the war. When we drove through town, we saw a lot of gold stars. And could not begin to imagine it could happen to our family.

"What are going to do?" cried Mom.

Dad said, "First of all we can't spend a dime in town unless we absolutely have to. We will eat all the vegetables you have canned in the pantry."

She had several jars of green beans and tomatoes Momma had canned.

"Son, we still have a few potatoes in the garden we haven't dug up yet. Dig up every single one. Even if some are little, they still taste good. Pick them all up and don't leave any! The hens are laying pretty good so we should have plenty of eggs. Those Yorkshire sows are worth some money, I'm sure I can find someone to buy them. We can eat the roosters and hens that are not laying. I can shoot a guinea or two if we have to, they taste pretty much like chicken. I can work at the plant, right up to the time I have to report for duty, and we should get pretty close to paying everything off."

Mom pulled me over next to her and said, "Where are we going to live?"

"I'll try and have enough money left to find a place to rent in town for a month or two. The government pays soldiers a little every month, I don't know how much. But I'll have it all sent home so you two should have enough to get by on."

It's one thing to get mad at your Dad for making you mind, it's another thing to realize that when he goes off to war, you might never see him again. I immediately got a bucket and the potato fork, then headed out back to start digging potatoes. I dug until dark and got every single one of them.

NARROW ESCAPE

With the loss of Midge and the rest of the cattle, we had to make the best of what our pigs might produce. Dad owned two sows. Both had just delivered piglets. One delivered seven, the other nine. These sows were big! White Yorkshire. Weighed about five hundred pounds each. The tiny pigs were cute. It was my job to take feed out to the sows in the morning. Watching the piglets nursing and having their breakfast was a cute thing to observe. I would have loved to pick one up, but I knew better. If a piglet started squealing the old sow would charge like a freight train. Just like a sow bear does when one of its cubs are endangered with the same possible result. I would normally walk casually through the lot, spreading out feed, then back to the gate on to the house and wash up before breakfast.

The little piglets, white with pink noses, were just venturing out this morning, on an exploration mission. Cute! As I was watching them, I noticed one little piglet venture close to the pond that backed up into the edge of the pig lot. As he was walking along the edge, he stepped his tiny rear right leg into the cold water. He'd never felt cold water before, and it scared him. He squealed as loudly as if the big bad wolf was just about to eat him. I then heard the sow make a loud woof! I knew what that was. It was time for me to run for my life! The sow mistakenly thought I had one of her piglets and was coming for me with bad intentions. Running for all I was worth I looked back out of the corner of my eye and she was almost on me.

She could kill me! There was no way I could make it to the gate. I then noticed a small hole in the lower part our fence I might fit through. I dove for it, went through just in time as the big sow hit the fence right behind me! She was after me big time and dang near had me. After that, I was afraid to feed the pigs the few weeks we had left.

THE BIG TURTLE

During the days of World War II, there were hardships of all kinds. Everything was scarce. Even if you were lucky enough to have money, there often was nothing to buy. We lived on a farm, and seldom, especially now with Dad going to the war, had little money. Those without money or food targeted farmers as a pretty sure way of getting a Sunday meal, figuring farmers had always butchered a chicken, a pig, or other livestock for enough food to survive. Some were dead beats grafting for a free meal, others were pitiful and had virtually nothing, not even food.

The next Sunday morning, a day after Dad had received his induction papers, a beat-up pickup truck with three children riding in the back, drove up to the house. The father got out and mumbled something about being a distant relative. I could tell by Dad's facial expression the guy was lying. Dad had never seen or heard of the guy before in his life. It was a "give us a free meal" set up. The children were pale and thin, the mother looked drawn and sad, looking like she had the remnants of a black eye.

Men who are failures, sometimes blame their wives for their own shortcomings. Sad!

It was not uncommon during those times, especially just before noon on Sundays, to have unknowns drop in for a "visit." In truth, most were just hungry and wanted something to eat. Distant cousins popped in from everywhere. Mom acted sympathetic, Dad, knowing he would soon be going to war, was more sympathetic than usual and turning to Mom whispered, "Do we have enough food to feed these people? I can open a jar of tomatoes and green beans, and we do have some potatoes dug from the garden, but we don't have an ounce of meat except a few slices of bacon which is barely enough for our breakfast and for sure is not enough to feed these people."

Dad rubbed his chin for a moment, then turned to me and said, "Son! Go to the back shed, get out the minnow seine, take the seine and meet me at the pond. I'll be out shortly, and we'll see if we can't catch enough fish to make a meal."

I ran to the store shed and pulled out the minnow seine and carried it to the pond. The seine was about twenty feet long, had a cork along the top so the fish wouldn't get over the top, with lead sinkers on the bottom so they wouldn't go under.

We had used the seine before so when Dad got to the pond, I had already had it unrolled. He grabbed the drag pole for one and started wading out in deep water. I took the other pole and dragged the water where it was shallower as I couldn't swim. He made one wide swing and he started walking fast towards the bank and we dragged the seine on shore. There was quite a number of fish jumping up in the net, and one big turtle.

He said "Son, stay away from that turtle, he's a snapping turtle and will bite your finger right off if it gets a chance!"

We quickly put the fish in a bucket he had brought from the shed, Dad picked up the turtle by the tail and threw it back in the pond, and he and I immediately starting cleaning them for Mom to cook for our "guests" who had shown up unannounced or invited. The father of the family sat in a chair inside and never even offered to come out and help or do anything. Obviously, a dead beat. Dad's looks towards him was starting to get a little steely eyed.

Mom fried up the fish, we sat down to the table and the father of the family with great haste picked up his fork reached over and was starting to spear for himself the biggest fish on the plate. Dad immediately started returning thanks before he could get to the fish. Table manners tells a lot about a man. This fellow was selfish and greedy. Dad laid a steely eye on the man who paled a little at seeing Dad's displeasure. When giving thanks was over Dad purposely picked up the platter of fish and first offered it to the man's wife, then their children, then to Mom and me, took a fish for himself, and passed the remaining small fish to the deadbeat. The message was passed, and the message clearly understood. They left with only a hasty and insincere thank you from the father after the meal. Dad bore fools poorly!

The next day a man showed up to look over the two big Yorkshire sows and determine what he might offer Dad for them. Apparently, his farming son was with them. The son said, "Look Dad, there's fifteen pigs with these sows." This could work out for us. They didn't notice my being there and listening to the conversation. When Dad came home, I told him what they said. He nodded his head in understanding, went inside and called the farmer on the telephone. When he hung up, he looked at Mom and said, "They brought a good price!" He looked at me on the way out to the barn and patted me on the head. I think that meant thanks son!

Dad worked as many hours as he could get at the plant. They paid time and a half for overtime and Dad took every hour he could. The coming Saturday, he was offered to work the full day and he took it. We were getting there on raising the money for the bank. Dad was so exhausted he went to bed right after supper and slept through the night. The next morning, Mom had me go out to the hen's nests and collect eggs for breakfast. I brought in an even dozen. She smiled and said I've been saving those few slices of bacon we have to make us a Sunday morning omelet. These will do just fine.

Dad didn't awaken until ten the next morning. First time I'd seen him look rested since lightening had killed Midge and the calf's and received notice he had been inducted into the United States Army. While eating his omelet he looked up at Mom smiling and said "We're going to make it! If I can get in these two weeks of work, we'll have enough to pay off the bank and be able to rent you two a place to live in town for at least two months with enough groceries to eat."

A little after that, as Dad was just finishing his last cup of coffee, a run-down car drove up with several kids in the back. Four of them, all red headed. It was just about eleven o'clock of course.

"Gosh dang it," said Dad. "The last thing we need right now is another one of those freeloaders coming to eat what little food we have."

He looked out the window a moment then said, "Well I'll be danged it if that's not Rufe Hawkins."

I peeked alongside of Dad and there was a tall red haired, freckle faced fellow, limping on one leg headed for our door.

Before he could knock, Dad opened the door and said "Hi Rufe! What brings you up this way?"

"Howdy Alf. Well I'll tell you the truth, me and my family is hungry, and we thought you might could give us something to eat. One of the cured tile stacks fell on my leg at the factory awhile back and since I can't do the work I used to do; they won't hire me back. It's been awful tough, and it wasn't my fault Alf."

"I know it wasn't. I heard about it and they didn't treat you right, that's for sure! Come on in and have a seat Rufe and my wife will go and invite your family in."

Dad looked at Rufe a minute and asked, "Can you pull a minnow seine?"

"I suppose I could. Whatcha got in mind."

"We have a pond out here that might have enough fish left in it to make us a meal if we seined it good and hard."

Rufe got up out of his chair and said, "Then let's have a go at it!"

Dad and Rufe walked out to the pond and I ran to the storehouse to get the seine.

Dad picked up the seine pole and started to go out into the deep water. Rufe looked at me, took my drag pole. "I'll take this one son!"

I liked Rufe. Picking up the seine pole he said, "Alf, I'm taller than you are so let me go out in the deep water and maybe we can catch some extra fish. There's three of you and six of us."

They made one sweep of the seine and came up with only eight small fish. Rufe said "Well let's try again."

They got about twelve small fish this time.

"Still not enough for a meal, Rufe."

"Let's try one more time I'm going to walk out into the deepest water on the other side, maybe we can have better luck there."

He and Dad pulled the seine over a good part of the pond and Dad said, "It's pulling pretty hard this time, we must have something in there."

They pulled the seine out on the bank and did have something in there for sure. Another ten or twelve small fish and the big snapping turtle.

"We're sure going to feed you and your family Rufe with canned vegetables and some fresh dug potatoes we have, but as you can see all we have is these few fish and no other meat to offer."

"You've got plenty of meat to offer Alf!"

Dad looked puzzled so Rufe added, "I can dress this big turtle out slicker than a whistle, there's a lot of meat there, and with these small fish we'll have plenty to eat."

Dad reached down and grabbed the turtle by the tail and did not throw him back in the pond this time. He carried him at arm's length away from his leg as a turtle that size could bite out a pretty big hunk of leg.

Rufe said "Alf do you have a hatchet?"

"Yes I do"!

"Good! Bring that out here and a good sharp knife and I'll show you how to dress out a turtle." He turned to me and said, "Go out under that tree there and bring me back a stick about two or three feet long. Make sure it's good and stout and at least an inch or two thick, we don't want it to break."

Was he going to hit the turtle? The shell so was so big and thick I didn't see how that would phase that big turtle a bit. This was really puzzling.

Dad had sat the turtle down on the grass to go inside and Rufe looked up and said, "Look at that ugly thing trying to crawl away. Keep your little dog away from it as it could bite it's leg right off!"

Snapping turtles must be wicked! I found a good size stick, showed it to Rufe, who said "That'll do just fine." He picked up the turtle by its tail and placed it on top of a big tree stump we had in the yard. It had been a big tree and the turtle was so big its shell covered a good part of the stump. When Dad came back Rufe asked, "Alf, hold on to the knife and let me have the hatchet. Is it good and sharp?"

"It's sharp."

Rufe then took the stick I had brought him, got out in front of the turtle and poked it in the nose a time or two. In a flash that turtle's head came from under the shell and bit the end of the stick. It had a BIG mouth and you could see the way the upper and lower jaws were formed, that it could bite your finger off in a second. This thing was scary. Rufe pulled the stick away, but with considerable effort, because the turtle kept snapping and biting at the stick like a mad dog.

Rufe then handed me the stick and said, "Here's what I want you to do. Come over here in front of the turtle."

With slow trepidation I walked over by Rufe and he handed me the stick. What was I supposed to do with it? He then said to Dad, "Hold its tail and keep it in place so it won't move."

Then he turned to me and said, "That old turtle is good and mad. Hold this stick out on the ends far away enough so it can't bite you, then put the middle of the stick right in front of his nose and he'll bite that stick so fast you won't even see it, and he will hold on to it too! When he's got it bit good and hard then pull the stick back towards you. He won't let go and you'll be able to stretch his old neck out quite a way. Your Dad's holding his tail on the opposite end, so you'll be safe. Got it?"

"Got it." And I was scared too!

Rufe picked up the hatchet and stood to the side by the turtle. I made sure my hands were on the farthest ends of the stick then I slowly moved the middle of the stick closer to the turtle's nose that was just peeking out from under the shell. When I got just a couple inches away from his nose that thing snapped out and bit the stick so fast and with such a vengeance it scared the heck out of me.

At the same time Rufe said, "Pull!"

I remembered and started pulling the stick back towards me. That turtle wouldn't let loose so I kept pulling and was stretching his neck out pretty far, and it still wouldn't let loose. Suddenly, the flash of the hatched blade came down and with one hard whack Rufe cut that turtle's head right off. I was pulling so hard I sat down backwards on the grass, still holding the stick with the turtle's head biting down in the middle of the stick.

Dad said, "Throw that stick away from you! His head is still alive and could still take off a finger."

I threw it over the fence into the pasture next door and took Frisky inside so she wouldn't go investigating what it was and get her nose bit off.

Rufe then took Dad's skinning knife, cut around the shell and it lifted right off. Under the shell, surprisingly there was a lot of meat! When he finished dressing the turtle he turned to Dad and said, "See Alf, I told you we had plenty to make a nice meal!" And, we did!

The last week before Dad left, the farm was practically barren. Dad had sold our milk cow, the chickens, sows and pigs, plus all the farm tools we had. It was two days before he would pick up his last paycheck from the plant, go in town and pay off the bank what he owed them. All we had left in the house to eat were crackers, two quarts of tomatoes, a large sack of Stark Delicious apples, and a big jar of peanut butter.

Mom had completed packing our clothes. We didn't have a lot. Just before noon on Thursday, she looked particularly sad. Dad was going off to war next week, leaving her and me alone in half of a little rented house with enough money for groceries to last for two months. I looked on the dinner table and saw slices of apples with peanut butter on them, placed in a circle around the edges of a plate. She was trying to make it appear as attractive as she could. Four peanut butter and crackers were placed in the center. That was it! That's all she had to put on the table. Knowing how sad she must be, I tried to think of something that might cheer here up.

Waiting until she was seated at the table I said, "Mom, what a beautiful plate, I do believe my favorite food of anything in this whole world is peanut butter and apples!" It was so obvious that I was trying to act like the ambassador of good cheer that she started crying and laughing at the same time. Apparently, my acting debut was not overly convincing. She dried her eyes and said, "Don't worry son, we'll get by."

Dad left Monday morning to face the unknown, maybe never to come back. Mom and I had a place to live and enough grocery money for two months. They say life is what you make it! Everything and everybody in this little town was new to me so I decided to get acquainted. I soon got to know most everyone in town and each day became a new adventure. I loved living in a small town where you get to know practically everybody, as well as their dog and cat! It's rather like living inside a big family. You get to know people on a close personal basis as compared to big city life where you know only the surface of what people care to reveal. I miss that genuine neighborhood life to this day. It was hard times on the one hand, yet a pleasant place to be a kid on the other!

BELATED CONFESSION

I never forgot that I told my first-grade teacher a lie when I was six years old! Actually five, as at the time, I was not yet six. She asked me if I knew what paste was, when I didn't. I was too embarrassed. It bothered me.

The little country one room schoolhouse where she taught for so many years closed, and our teacher, Mrs. Smith moved to town to teach the first and second grade. Thirty years later, I was driving through the little town where I grew up. Mrs. Smith was now retired. I found out where she lived, drove to her house and knocked on the front door. The tall dark haired first grade teacher now had hair as white as snow, and she wasn't tall at all. She was surprisingly petite. Just a little over five feet. I guess when you're six years old everybody is tall. She gave me a hug when she remembered who I was and bade me to sit down and tell her where all I'd been and what I'd done.

She asked, "Do you still sing?"

It just so happened one of the songs I'd recorded was on the juke box at the local restaurant.

"A little," I said.

After about fifteen minutes of visitation I told her why I was here.

"I've come to make a confession."

"Why what on earth could that be?"

"On my very first day of school, you gave me a small cut out picture of a Jersey cow, a big sheet of red paper, and said 'Take this paste and put the cow on the red paper.' Then you said, 'You do know how to paste don't you?' I said 'Yes, I do,' but I had never seen a bottle of paste in my life. So, I lied to you my first day of school and it's bothered me all these years."

She then got up from her chair, walked across the room and said "How incredible! I've never experienced anything like this in my life."

We chatted a while longer about our life's journey. When I stood up to leave, she gave me warm motherly hug and said, "You're forgiven my child, heaven knows you're completely forgiven."

Suddenly, I felt six years old again. "Thank you, Mrs. Smith!"

What a sweet lady she was. How lucky I was that a kind lady of such character would come into my life. Hopefully dear teacher you're now playing piano with the angels in heaven. If so, sweet lady, stroke the keys a little more gently if you please.

FATHER BOB, FRANCISCAN PRIEST

"There's something in the air!"

If you've traveled throughout the world as much as I have, met multitudes of people from all walks of life, in many countries, you recognize an exceptional person when you meet one. Father Bob was one of those persons.

He had served as a priest in the Amazon and South Africa as well as other far off places for several years. He had seen it all, lived and breathed it all, caught malaria and still had the depth of faith and courage to bring peace and joy to those most in need. Rome then recognized his abilities and called him to serve there as General Secretariat of the missions for several years. Other priests referred to him as "One of the great ones."

While writing this, I'm reminded once again, of how great he was. I have a photo of him on my office wall, meeting Pope John Paul II. Now Saint John Paul II! I have another photo of him sitting and visiting with Mother Teresa in Calcutta. Lastly, the final picture is of him holding mass at her tomb, after she had passed away. He sent me one of her cards he had received from her earlier, that included her signature. It's hard to believe, I have the signature of a saint hanging on my office wall. Father Bob indeed was "One of The Great Ones!"

When we first met, he was a Priest at St. Maria Goretti. After attending his mass services a few times, I asked for an appointment. I explained that I felt that I had been doing fairly well as a Christian but needed to bring it on up a notch. A hoed garden doesn't stay hoed! During our meeting he said, "Go home and forgive yourself of every wrong thing you've ever done for three days. Then don't do it again!"

The human mind records memory via how recent, how frequent, and how intense something crosses your mind. In these past years, whenever I have thought of Father Bob, what has come to mind is an intense scene where a small girl, eight years old or so, all dressed up in a beautiful white gown, veil and white shoes, is walking up to receive the host for her confirmation. It was plain to see that she is quite ill, with an unhealthy complexion. Her right leg had been removed and she was walking courageously with a prosthetic leg with a little white shoe on it as well.

She laboriously made her way down the aisle, and every step up to the podium was a struggle. Every parishioner turned their attention to her and was praying for her every step. Father Bob bent down ever so tenderly, and delivered her the host, doing his best to give her all the love and hope he could. Everyone in the filled church realized her time was very short. The courage and commitment she expressed was an inspiration to all of us. Handkerchiefs were brought out throughout the church, dabbing at tear filled eyes and sniffling noses. That touching scene always comes to mind whenever I think of Father Bob.

While he was still our beloved Father at St. Maria Goretti, my wife Betty reminded me one Sunday morning after mass, that the Knights of Columbus were having a breakfast and raffle in one of the halls. Catholics do things like that. I had already chartered course for another establishment, but quickly did a U-turn and went back to support the efforts of our church and say hello to some people we might know. I was hoping Father Bob would be there. "Great ones" don't come by every day!

It was nearing the end of breakfast by the time we got there, and not many breakfast servings were left. I noticed the line of raffle ticket buyers was thinning out, so I rushed up, ordered breakfast, and bought raffle tickets for cakes, wine, and various other prizes. In a few minutes, they announced the winners and I was astonished that I had won several of them. The last thing I bought were six tickets for five dollars, sponsored by American Airlines. The winner would receive two free tickets to Europe. Drawings would be made late in the afternoon. Over six thousand tickets were sold. I wrote my phone number on the back of the tickets and expected to hear no more from them.

Betty had a Cookie Bouquet franchise at the time, as she is an incredible baker. My contribution to her was to clean up the shop on Sunday afternoons, so she could walk into a tidy and clean establishment on Monday mornings. Her work was long and challenging and I know she appreciated what help I could give. A couple hours into my cleaning the phone rang. Since she closed her shop on Sundays, I answered the phone, presuming it was her wanting me to bring home something from the grocery store next door.

When I answered it was sure enough her, and she said: "Are you sitting down?"

"No! Not exactly! I'm holding a mop in my right hand."

"Well here it is, you won the trip for two to Europe."

Thinking her joking of course, I said, "Sure, what is it you want from the store?"

"No! I'm not kidding! They want you to come over for pictures."

"Holy mackerel! If you're not kidding, where in Europe do you want to go?"

"Rome, of course!"

So, Rome it was!

We had breakfast with Father Bob the morning before we left for Rome. Because of all that he had done, seen, and experienced, there was a presence about him that made you realize you were in the company of someone special. I hopefully asked if he might know of some of his fellow priests in Rome who would offer suggestions on where we should go and what we should see. He said he did and would email them that we were coming. "By the way", he added, "while you're in Rome, take the train a few short miles up north to Assisi! There's something in the air there!" With that he raised his right index finger in the air and circled it around. He added nothing else. How mysterious I thought!

I wanted to ask what he meant by that, but decided that you don't question a priest who slept on native mats while in the Amazon, ate whatever food was available, caught malaria, then went on to South Africa, and other places for years on end, speaking fluently in several languages as he went, a whole lot of trivial questions. He was, so to speak, a religious heavy! We said we would definitely go! And we did!

Was he ever right about something being in the air in Assisi! Wow! Thank you, Father Bob! You knew of which you spoke!

ROME

Rome, the eternal city, is an awesome place. After a lifetime of seeing pictures of the ancient coliseum, and then looking at it in person only a few blocks away, seemed surreal. It felt like we were in a dream!

Eager, smiling faced tourists, holy men, and pickpockets, all mingling together in a seemingly never-ending throng of humanity added another layer of surrealism. Father Bob had instructed us to take a cab from the airport to the Franciscan Monastery, give them Father Bob's name, and ask if they could be of assistance.

Finding a hotel for the night, and a map of suggested key sights, would be of great benefit.

The cabbie dropped us off a couple blocks from the monastery. Not exactly sure which of the buildings was the monastery, we were relieved to see a priest walking just across the narrow street from where we were standing. I called out:
"Are you a Franciscan?"
"Are you the Wassons?" He answered back.

Wow! Father Bob had indeed contacted the Monastery! What a relief! The priest was short in stature and brilliant of mind. He introduced himself as Father Adalbert. It was the day after Easter. He asked where we were staying. I said we had been trying to find a room with no success. He informed us there was not a single room left in Rome due to the Easter celebration, and very grumpily, he added, "I guess we will have to put you up for the night."

That was a relief, feeling humble for not having more travel foresight.

"Thank you Father, we certainly appreciate your hospitality."

The "we" he referred to would be the seven other priests that were in residence at the time.

Having been raised on a farm, milking cows, feeding chickens and livestock, sleeping the night in a Franciscan Monastery, in Rome, was beyond my imagination. My wife Betty, our son Bryan, and I were most grateful shelter seekers. Father Adalbert first took me to a large unheated room, with tall ceilings and a cot for a bed.

"One of our Bishops slept here last night."

Franciscans are known for their frugality. On the way out he said, "By the way, this room was once Caesar's pharmacy."

Wow! That's a lot of history! I later found out there was no heated water in their showers either.

Betty and Bryan were to sleep in other rooms down the hall. He then turned to our son Bryan and said, "I understand you're a doctor."

"Yes, I am, how can I help you?"

"I'm having leg pains, could you see what the cause might be?"

Bryan recognized his problem, which was easily solved and sent him some pressure stockings after returning home. Before he showed Betty and Bryan their rooms he paused, turned and said, "I think we have enough ice cream tonight for everyone. Would you care to dine with us?"

Once again, those blessed men are quite frugal. "Well of course, what time?"

"Six, in the dining hall. Someone will show you the way."

Staying in a monastery that's centuries old, is an awesome experience. At six p.m. we were shown the way to the dining hall. As we entered the large room with tall ceilings, we nodded to the eight solemn priests, including Father Adalbert, who all sat on the same side of one long table facing us. To our right were two elderly ladies, stirring a pot of soup, and preparing the remainder of the meal. We sat in the middle off to one side. The soup was served, and we didn't know whether to return our own thanks and start to eat or what. Then all at once our question was answered. The eight priests, in unison began singing a Gregorian chant.

Their voices, in splendid unison, rose to the tall ceiling, filling the room with such an incredible holy sound. Spiritually beautiful! It practically made your hair stand on end. Stunned, we sat there looking and drinking in this once in a lifetime experience. It was one of those "come to Jesus" moments they talk about. I had already followed Father Bob's advice of forgiving myself of all wrongs for three days. It might be a good time and the right place to double down on that one. We had never witnessed anything like hearing Gregorian chants up close and in person, and I'm sure, never will again. It was such a beautiful, deeply moving, spiritual evening! It's still hard to comprehend, and awesome to remember!

I had been to Rome three times before, but when an intelligent religious historical scholar, like Father Adalbert, started escorting us to the various historical sites, I realized I had never really seen it! Not even close! Of the countless historical facts, he revealed, the memory about Bernini comes to mind.

Bernini produced the greatest sculptures of the 17th century. He is known for developing the Baroque style of art. The revered Three Fountains in Rome, seen by millions, are only one of his many creations. Apparently one of the Popes was a bit of a tightwad and was slow on paying for the art he had ordered. On the very bottom of one of Bernini's sculptures, quite tiny so as not to be noticed by the Pope, Bernini sculptured several small lizards. Sculpture rebellion! Father Adalbert's innumerable intricate tales were another once in a lifetime Rome experience, not likely to come our way again.

On one occasion, he was taking us to see a carved wooden display showing in detail just how Roman life was lived in the 4th century. A perceptive Roman Senator's wife, thinking of the future, had commissioned tiny wooden carvings, depicting in detail, the daily lives that reflected their time period. One could get a glimpse of each household and their different daily activities: Tiny carved chickens kept in tiny carved cages for the next day's meal, ladies cooking over fires, hanging out clothes to dry, dogs in the street. The daily activities of two hundred households or more were depicted in these miniature carvings. After seeing this amazing and informative feat of art, I felt I understood how Roman citizens lived on a day-by-day basis back then. How wonderfully thoughtful of the futuristic thinking Senator's wife to do so! The Senator might have had the political position, but it was she who had the better intuition for those of us who would follow. Thank you, kind lady!

On the way to view this wonderful display, we walked through an area where young girls worked. Apparently one of the young ladies' gray and white cat had eaten a poisoned mouse. The cat on the floor, looked like it was a goner. Its eyes had already set in its head. She tugged at father's robe as he walked by and repeated two or three times "Please padre, bless my gatto (Italian for cat)!" He shooed her away saying he wasn't going to bless any cat. After viewing the miniature display, we went on by ourselves to view other sights and Father Adalbert went back the way we had come. I don't know for sure, but suspect Father Adalbert softened up and blessed the cat on the way back through, or not. The next morning, we passed back through that same area. To our surprise the would be dead gray and white cat, was bouncing around as pretty as you please. Never underestimate the power of prayer!

Father Adalbert's detailed explanation of the lives represented by the wooden carved figures in the display, made the lives of those in the past practically come alive. Father Adalbert too is now gone. I was told he was found on his knees at the edge of his bed with the holy Rosary tucked in his hands under his head. He always reminded us when we parted to say a couple Hail Mary's when we thought of him. We did Father. Just now! I know you prayed for us as well! Thank you!

I must share this last fond memory that I carry in my heart of Father Adalbert. We quickly discovered that we both shared a love for music. Surprisingly, he loved to sing the old standard popular songs. He knew every word! Once he found out I was a singer songwriter, he insisted I sing along with him, which we did for hours! During this moment, the priest simply became a man in my eyes, and I was glad I could bring him such joy. What a privilege to have known him and sang songs with him!

SAINT FRANCIS OF ASSISI

After three days of touring, I recalled Father Bob's suggestion of taking the train up to Assisi. Something was in the air there! Father Adalbert called ahead and planned for us to stay at the American Franciscan Nuns Hotel. A small place, spotless throughout, ran by elderly, flower sweet nuns. One simple meal a day at lunchtime was served. You had to sign up in advance. There was no wasting of food there. Wouldn't want to anyway as it was delicious; as was every minute we spent in Assisi!

The city Saint Francis grew up in is a small beautiful place, on the side of an Italian mountain. Proud owners keep the city tidy and clean. Rumors were that no family had ever sold their property to an outsider, in the past seven hundred years. Their globally recognized St. Francis, whose miracles and influence led to the formation of the Franciscan priests scattered throughout much of the world, was indeed a citizen to be proud of. Father Bob and Father Adalbert were both Franciscans.

I had a bad cold and the warm, toasty, spotless rooms of the American San Franciscan Nuns Hotel was a blessing. The aging nuns were as sweet as honey. My son, Dr. Bryan Lee's good humor, made them laugh until they begged him to stop. The next morning, the three of us went out for breakfast. Betty and I walked through some of the toyshops while our son Bryan went to the church. I purchased a delightful wooden Pinocchio with a long red nose.

Bryan came back and said, "You need to go to the church. The tomb of Saint Francis is on the second level down. You need to go there!" As Betty and I walked the cobble stoned street towards the church, the wonderful aroma of Italian tomato sauce filled the air. She smiled at me with a knowing look that meant she knew I wanted something Italian for lunch. She was right! So, did she!

I have been in many countries throughout the world. In nearly all of them you will see The Saint Francis Prayer hanging on some wall or featured in some book or placard. To be in the same city where he was born and lived, and walking the same streets he walked, gave us a rather airy feeling. His prayer is sung in many churches, throughout the world. Nice melody with a timeless message!

> "Where there is hatred let me sow love. Where
> there is injury, pardon. Where there is doubt, faith.
> Where there is despair, hope. Where there is darkness,
> light. Where there is sadness, joy."

Who living in this world could find fault with that?

There were several tall straight-backed chairs sitting in front of his tomb. Eight or ten I would say. Walking up to the tomb, I was surprised to see the bones of St. Francis, right in front of me, neatly laid out in clinical fashion with skeletal bones, exposed, and perfectly displayed except for his skull. He was apparently small in stature. Not knowing what else to do I sat in the front row directly in front of his tomb. I said a prayer and relaxed, letting the gravity of the moment sink in. In a moment or two, slowly, but very noticeably, I started feeling an energy source coming through from his tomb.

It was confusing, unlike anything I had ever felt before. It reminded me somewhat of walking in a misty fog, where you think you can feel the light sensation of moisture on your skin, but upon wiping your hand across your forehead, feel no evidence of moisture. It was then I remembered that Saint Francis had penetrated, broken through, been recognized, or had been spoken to, by the higher power we call God. I had always believed God existed, except for only the slightest smidgen of doubt, which I couldn't quite shake. When the energy of his power is being transferred right to your face through the tomb of Saint Francis, you no longer doubt his presence! He is right there in front of you! When I rose from my chair and walked away, the weight of the moment unsteadied me a bit. This was big! It was a life changing experience for me! I never quite thought the same way about religion again. From then on, I simply believed! No doubt at all! It's a comforting feeling!

Someday, if you get a chance to go to Rome, take the train for a short ride on up to Assisi. When you get there, sit down in front of the tomb of Saint Francis. Relax a moment or two, and you'll discover what Father Bob meant when he said, "Go on up to Assisi, there's something in the air there!" Yes, there is Father Bob.

A young lady alongside me on a treadmill at a gym a few years later, remarked she had just returned from Italy.
"By chance, did you go on up to Assisi?"
She said she had! Then she remarked, "You know that's really a holy place up there!"
Well, what do you know! She too must have discovered that in Assisi, there is "something in the air!"

SIDESTEP - POSITIVE MESSAGES

As a child, then later as a young man, I often listened to the sermons of the esteemed Dr. Billy Graham. He was a great man of God as well. Today, I often listen to Joel Osteen. Dearly love his positive, uplifting messages. I've noticed, and I believe it to be borne out statistically, that families of faith are happier, healthier, live longer, and tend to do better overall. Sounds to me like a pretty good reason to go to church somewhere and give thanks for our blessings.

GOODNIGHT MISS RUBY

There's a memory of a sweet lady that has found a permanent place in my mind and heart. The loneliness of it saddens me still.

Miss Ruby was a petite little woman, who wore dark clothes most of the time. Although old in years, her hair untouched by the paintbrush of time, remained black and always neatly tied in a bun in back.

I often saw her walking past Mom and my little rented duplex in the evening, going to town to buy herself one piece of candy. She always bought just the one piece of chocolate. Couldn't afford any more. She had no one! Her husband had died years ago, no children, and no relatives of any kind ever showed up at her door. She was completely alone.

As poor as she was, she never let on. Never asked for anything. She walked with a quiet dignity, spoke softly and always with a polite trace of a smile. A lonely smile as I recall. I would always say,
"Hi Miss Ruby!"
"Good evening, how are you this evening son?"
"I'm fine Miss Ruby!"
I liked her! She had a soft peaceful way about her.

Meat was scarce in those days! Everyone knew Miss Ruby had nothing but a few dollars and the little patch of garden where she grew vegetables. Neighbors would drop by now and then say "Miss Ruby! I got this big old chicken and we can't possibly eat all of it, could you do us a favor and take a piece or two of it off our hands." She would cordially smile and softly remark, "I would be most glad to help out!" They would mostly give her the neck and backs. Barely having enough for their own families, it was still a sacrifice. Nearly everyone in our neighborhood would take her a little meat from time to time.

One evening as she was walking by where Mom and I lived, she stopped, turned to me and said, "Hi son, how are you doing this evening?"

She never did much more than just smile and nod.

Surprised I answered, "Why fine Miss Ruby, how are you?"

"Never felt better, I'm walking up to the drug store to buy me a piece of chocolate candy. How would you like to come along, and I'll buy you one too!"

"Why I'd love that Miss Ruby!"

Wow, she was going to buy two pieces!

She held out her hand and took mine in hers. Another surprise! We walked hand in hand on our way up to the drug store. I'd never seen her hold hands with anybody before. Her hand was warm and gentle to the touch. I felt very special. She said she had always loved chocolate candy ever since she was a little girl. Chuckling she said, "Some parts of us never quite grow up you know." As we walked into the drug store, she stepped up to the candy display, took out a small black snap coin purse, removed two nickels, and ordered two-star shaped chocolate kisses. She took one and handed me another, then dropped the small coin purse into the wastebasket at the door on the way out.

When I gave her a puzzled look she smiled and patted me on the head and said, "I won't be needing that silly old thing anymore!"

As we came to my house, she let go of my hand, looked at me with a soft smile, brushed the hair out of my eyes, and said "You're going to grow up to be a fine young man. May you have a happy life and bring much happiness to others." With that, she did the most unusual thing, she leaned over and kissed me on my forehead. As she turned and walked away, I said, "Goodnight Miss Ruby, and thank you for the candy!" Not looking back, she raised her left hand acknowledging goodbye, and walked off into the twilight.

"Where've you been son?" Mom asked as I walked in the door.
"Walked with Miss Ruby up to the drug store! She bought me a star candy kiss out of the candy case and kissed me on my forehead goodnight!"
"Why my goodness, never heard of her doing such a thing."

The two o'clock night train, that regularly ran through town, always just let out one train whistle, knowing nobody in our little town would be up that late. However, that night the train whistle blew and blew. Sleepy residents presumed some neighbors' milk cow must have wondered onto the tracks.

The next morning Mom had scrambled me one egg for breakfast, along with a slice of toast and homemade tomato preserves, a treat she knew I dearly loved. "Thanks Mom" I said, munching away and noticing that it had frosted during the night. The sun's bright rays made the frozen dewdrops glisten like diamonds. I picked up my homework reading book, tucked it under my arm and started off for school.

My route was to walk two blocks to the right of our house, one block to the left past the shop keeper's store, cross the railroad tracks past the train depot and then four more blocks straight to school. I would normally only see a couple classmates at the railroad crossing, going in the same direction as me, nothing else.

But this morning was different! There were several people gathered around. The depot master was standing at the tracks, talking to the townspeople in a hushed tone. He was having a serious conversation with Kenneth the feed storeowner, and Bill the barber.

"As you know, the two o'clock train comes right through here every night at the same time. It never stops, so it goes through town at a high speed. The engineer said last night at two o'clock, as he was entering town, a small woman, dressed in black, with dark hair made up in a bun in back, stepped out onto the tracks. She just kept on slowly walking down the middle of the track, in the same direction as the train. He blew the train whistle at least a dozen times for her to get off, but she just kept walking on, real slow. The train hit her, right here in front of the depot."

"Miss Ruby!" I shouted out, as I just knew in my heart that it had to be her.

They turned to me with drawn faces, nodded, and from their expression, I knew the answer. I couldn't believe it! I made my way around the crowd and walked on the tracks in front of the depot. At a young age, I was already an experienced hunter and started looking for signs. Smatterings of blood, small cranial fragments, along with some traces of black hair, were scattered on both sides of the rails told the story. It broke my heart to see!

Looking ahead about twenty feet, a cur dog was licking something in the middle of the track. I shooed the dog away and picked up a handful of rocks and threw them at him. Bending down to see, I saw that it was the complete intact frontal lobe from inside Miss Ruby's skull. I called over to the depot master, he came, and I showed him what I'd found. He said he would take care of it. I threw more rocks as hard as I could at the cur dog to shoo him further away. Then went on to school.

For some reason, witnessing Miss Ruby's remains scattered over the tracks didn't bother me much. Her remains were not the warm kind person I walked with hand in hand on the way to the drug store last night. Miss Ruby had gone away to be somewhere else. The thing that haunts me still, about the passing of Miss Ruby, is how desperately lonely and frightened she must have felt, as she stepped out onto the tracks, in front of the two o'clock night train. Hearing the train coming down the track, and the engineer, seeing this little woman dressed in black with her hair tied up in a bun, slowly walking in front of him. His frantic blowing of the loud train whistle must have been deafening. The ground vibration of the thundering train bearing down upon her would have been an awful thing to experience. The petite, quiet, soft-spoken little woman with her dark hair neatly rolled up in a bun in back, never flinched a step from her intended mission. Walking along slowly, down the middle of the railroad track, perhaps reliving some of her most precious memories, Miss Ruby softly walked off into eternity!

To this day, when I'm walking through a crowd, and see a dark-haired petite woman, with a bun tied up in back, I pause a moment and think fondly of Miss Ruby. The overwhelming loneliness and desperation she felt that night, must have been more than her poor heart could stand. She was a kind and gentle woman. "Good night Miss Ruby and thank you for the chocolate candy kiss! God bless you sweet lady, and may you rest in peace!

STANLEY AND ME

It was a cold November day and two inches of soft winter snow had blanketed the plains of Missouri in the early morning. By four thirty in the afternoon, school had let out, the temperature raised above freezing, turning the snowy white blanket into a muddy mixture of ice and water. Small children in those days wore rubber overshoes, the buckle up kind, that you put over your school shoes to keep them from getting wet.

It was just before the Army called my Dad off to war and we were still living on the farm, three and a half miles from town. Mom asked us to go to town and buy flour and sugar at the grocery store, along with a pound of bacon, if they had it. Groceries were rationed. It was war time, 1942, and our fighting soldiers overseas had to be fed and supplied first.

The first time I became aware of Stanley, his visual presence was preceded by the sound of loud crying of childhood displeasure. His Dad's grocery store was our destination. Out of curiosity, I walked around the end of the sparsely stocked counter, to see from whom the sound was originating. Standing by the cash register, a smallish tearful blue-eyed boy, cap earflaps sticking out on both sides, was informing the world, that, in his opinion, he had been wrongfully spanked. He appeared to be about my age, seven or eight. As he cried on, my eyes fell to his overshoes. They were buckled up and pointing in opposite directions. He had apparently put each overshoe on the wrong foot.

Dad tapped me on the shoulder and said, "It's time to go". He had a sack of flour in his hand, but no sugar or bacon. Because of his considerable physical power, and often willingness to use it, I quickly responded. Turning to go, I looked back at the boy who decibel wise had been turned up to a high volume. He stopped crying for a moment as we made eye contact. He sniffled hard but wasn't about to cry further in front of the new boy that had just come into their store. I looked again at his wrong foot overshoes, a problem I'd experienced a time or two myself, went out the door and got into the car. There was some ice on the road home and Dad drove with slow caution. He never talked to me much when I was a child, so I sat there in silence thinking to myself as we rode along. I wondered about the crying boy and made a mental note to make sure I put my overshoes on the right foot. I later learned Stanley was his name. Soon after, my Dad was called off to war and Mom and I moved to town. Stanley and I became pals, enjoyed tons of boyhood experiences together, and in the process became lifelong friends. These are our some of our more memorable adventures, as well as an individual or two of mine.

THE RED FOX

At the age of ten Stanley and I were brave hunters, trappers of furbearing critters, and all-around explorers of the great American outdoors. His Dad had given him a used pump .22 rifle, with a V sight in front, hexagon barrel. It shot only short rifle cartridges as I recall. I had come by a well-used single shot 410 shotgun, from my grandfather. Shot either 2 ½" or 3" inch shells. I loved that gun, and I could dang sure shoot with it! With that arsenal we could take on just about anything on the planet.

It was November, trapping season, and my Dad had given me one spring steel trap for my adventure into trapping while he was away in the army. I had often read "how to trap" books at the local barber shop while waiting for my quarterly haircut.

About a mile east of town, the eastern wind blew in a scent that reminded our little town that a family of skunks was denned up at a pond dam near there. Stanley and I, wannabe trappers that we were, caught that scent. We investigated and discovered from the local trappers that skunk hides would bring in as much as seven dollars each. Skunk coats for some reason, had become quite fashionable with the fine ladies of New York. Seven dollars was a kid's fortune in those days. Candy bars and soda pop were a nickel each. The decision was made to become skunk trappers!

Early one Saturday we took my one steel trap and headed for the pond where the skunks' den was dug into the side of the pond dam. A sizeable entrance hole, surrounded by small shrubs, was our obvious target.

I brought from home a three-foot length of wire to tie onto the trap chain, secured it around one of the stronger shrubs, stretched out the wire and chain conglomeration far enough to place the trap right in front of the entrance to the den.

Neither of us had ever set a trap before so it turned out to be a rather finger pinching experience. After some trial and error, we discovered that if one of us stood on the trap springs, the other could set the trigger of the trap without getting pinched, and we would have all our fingers in good condition when we returned home. The trap was finally put in place and we concluded it was picture perfect. We covered the trap very delicately with leaves and proudly started for home. Glory was just a day away!

When we awoke Sunday morning, the Missouri prairie was once again covered with a pristine blanket of snow. Since there was no school, it was a play day, and kids hurriedly ate breakfast and ran to their store-sheds to bring out their sleds. Checking the trap would have to wait. This was a father and son day!

The custom at the time was that our fathers would produce a long length of rope, tie the rope to the sled, loop the rope through the back bumper of the car and give the remaining end of the rope to the child to hold on to. Dads would then pull their children on their sleds, throughout the small town behind the family car at a merry pace. Huge fun!

There's always a downside to everything. Even on a fun filled snowy day when fathers are pulling children around town on their sleds.

SIDESTEP: BLUE WESTERN FLYER

The little country town where Stanley and I grew up had a population of five hundred and seventy-eight. Few afforded television, however most had radios and radio news of the war was scary. Freedom to kids from all the bad news was their bike. My beloved grandma Bessie bought me my first bicycle. Saved up her egg money to buy it. Her Rhode Island Red chickens were good layers! My bike was a blue Western Flyer. I loved it! The first day I had the bike, I learned how to ride it in a wobbly fashion. To my great pleasure, my aunt and her rich husband, drove up in a new baby blue Hudson Hornet. So anxious to see them, pedaling closely behind, I failed to stop when he did, and bumped right into the back of his brand-new car. They were unimpressed with both me, and my cycling skills.

Riding bikes from morning to night was our daily routine. A healthy outlet! In that exploratory process we learned, and knew, every dog and cat in town, and to whom it belonged. I've told large city people this and they find it unbelievable. But it's true.

SIDESTEP: SINGING HENS

Once at a gathering in New York City, surrounded by city dwellers, I mentioned to a lady raised in those confines of metropolitan life, that old hens sang. In utter disbelief she loudly exclaimed, "I don't believe that!" Knowing there was no way in the world I would ever convince her otherwise, I strolled over to a young painter who was showing his new creation to other guests, while she took up conversation with someone else. When she pointed me out across the room to her new conversationalist, I'm sure she was declaring me unbalanced. I passed on to another room full of guests and mostly listened the rest of the evening. However, anyone who has ever raised a flock of chickens knows that occasionally, not always, when an old hen lays an egg, she walks off her nest, happily singing a chicken song. Correction, hen song! Roosters do not sing!

SIDESTEP: DANCING PEACOCK

In later years, while on vacation in Maui, I went to see a peacock they said would dance if you gave him food. Doubtful indeed, I went to the refuge, saw three peacocks standing together, and wanting to find out if this was fact or fiction, held out a slice of bread. Sure enough, one came over and rapidly began raising his feet up and down. He stopped, I delivered, and he ate the bread. Then he rapidly started raising his feet up and down again in anticipation of more! I fulfilled my part of the bargain and gave him another slice for his outstanding performance! Two other peacocks, in the same holding area, less enterprising, didn't dance. They, of course, remained unfed. I once fed a dancing peacock on the island of Maui!

BACK TO THE RED FOX

The well-known Zarker dog was the scourge of small children in our little town. Every kid either knew or had heard tales of him. He was mostly white with a large tan spot around his right eye and one tan ear. Had bitten almost every kid in town. He would bare his teeth, and with bad intentions, utter a low fearsome growl, and chase after any kid who had the misfortune of riding by the Zarker house. If you could peddle fast enough, it was possible to outrun him. For some reason, he never barked. A stealth attack was his preference. Slower peddlers would be bitten on the leg or ankle, sometimes causing them to fall off their bikes and collect a few extra bites while down. I was a fast peddler and managed to outrun him by the very least little bit. Scared me to death each time! Every kid in town was afraid of and despised the Zarker dog. Me included.

My cheeks were getting red and cold from the brisk sled ride, but that was o.k. It was so thrilling to have my Dad pull me behind his car, through the snow-covered streets, and see him smiling and waving at neighbors as we went by. I wished he would always act that way.

Not being a bicycle kid, Dad wasn't aware of the dreaded Zarker dog's reputation. The town streets were laid out in a square, and Dad drove up and down each street methodically, smiling and waving. A happy time for us both! I was having so much fun myself, holding onto the rope with one hand and waving, that I hadn't noticed Dad was pulling me right in front of the dreaded Zarker dog's house. He was a fast runner, and the car's speed was casually slow.

My heart sank as a feeling of primal fear came over me, hoping against hope, the dastardly dog would not be at home. I hesitated to even look in their yard for fear his eyes would zero in on me! Wishful hopes are not always granted. There he was, standing right in the middle of the snow-covered yard! Some dogs have mean eyes, and he was a mean eyed dog if ever I saw one!

I couldn't help the heavy feeling of dread, as I looked at him. His angry eyes riveted on me and I saw him crouch. Without even a bark, he silently charged through the snow, coming for me at a full run. He never made a sound. He just attacked! I was in for it. Dad was not looking in the car's rear mirror and hadn't the slightest idea that the dog from hell was almost on me.

129

I then did the dumbest thing I could have done. I panicked, froze and let go of the rope. In slow motion, the rope seemed to have a life of its own, as it slowly went slack, while the car's rear bumper cruised away in the distance. My sled and I started moving slower and slower, as the length of rope played out, dropping in the snow and then pulled away behind dad's car. The beastly, Zarker dog was coming closer and closer as fast as he could run. The dread of knowing the inevitable is close by, and certain to happen, is indeed an awful feeling.

Up close, the dogs ugly face, with his long fangs bared, was dreadful to look at. Looking over my right shoulder, he appeared just inches behind my slowing sled, when he leaped, and bit me right square in the middle of the back.

Dad, finally looking in the car mirror, seeing I was rolling around in the snow trying to fend off the dog, turned the car around and came to my salvation. He kicked the dog off me, picked up my sled, and put us both in the back of the car. My back was bruised badly, but my heavy winter coat kept his teeth from breaking the skin. I was more scared than hurt, but pain and fear are strong emotions, long remembered.

By afternoon, my childhood fears had settled down and I decided to go up to the grocery store and see what Stanley was doing. He had been out building a snowman and was warming his hands by the fire.

When he saw me walking in, he said, "What have you been up to?"

"Dad took me sledding. Drove by the Zarker house and their dog got me!"

"Bit you?"

"Yeah, right in the middle of the back!"

"Bloody?"

"No, bit me through my coat. Bruised me up pretty good but didn't break the skin."

"Feelin' o.k.?"

"Yeah, I'm o.k."

"Then let's go out to the pond dam and see if we caught a skunk! Might shoot a rabbit along the way."

My courage returned instantly by the thought of a good hunt. "Sounds good to me! My house is on the way so why don't you get your rifle and we'll go to the trap from there."

"O.K." he said, "I'll be there in an hour."

The temperature was below freezing, and as we walked to the edge of town, the snow in the pasture was undisturbed and postcard picture perfect. We could see our breath as we walked. If you have never walked on freshly fallen snow, you should try it, there is nothing like it in the world, especially if the sun is out and makes the snow look like a field of the shiniest diamonds you'll ever see.

After a few minutes, the pond dam, where the skunks were denned, came into view. Stanley said, "Look how all that ground is torn up around that den, and something has chewed off the saplings all around it." I had been concentrating on looking for a rabbit near the fence line and hadn't looked in the direction of the dam. Wow! Black dirt completely covered the dam above the den where the skunks lived, ruining the white pristine landscape. The small saplings indeed were chewed in two, and even the lower bark, from the bigger trees, were chewed off at the bottom.

Stanley levered a cartridge into his rifle. I pulled back the hammer on my shotgun.

"Something's really big in that trap," Stanley whispered.

"Uh huh" I said, and shoulder to shoulder, as two soldiers going to battle, we walked over the edge of the dam, and looked down to the place where we'd set the trap.

To our surprise, the plume of a large red tail was waving in the air. We'd caught a red fox! The front half of the fox could not be seen as he had heard us coming and dug himself deep into the skunk hole. The back half was exposed, leaving his red tail sticking straight up. The beautiful red plume was gently waving back and forth in the cold winter breeze! However, there was no time to enjoy the colorful contrast of the red plume with the white snow in the field beyond, as the fox was still very much alive and caught in our trap. Being equipped with large teeth that had proven they could bite small trees in half was a rather sobering prospect to face.

Fox are one of the smartest wild animals, very hard to catch, and only the old-time trappers knew how to catch one. How we had caught this smart fox was a puzzle! I looked back to the edge of the den. A rabbit track in the snow led straight from the field toward the skunk den. Fox tracks were right behind. That was the answer! The fox had been chasing the rabbit, which was running for his life for the hole in the skunk den. The freshly fallen snow had covered and concealed the trap. Diving for the hole, the lucky rabbit had jumped over the trap and the cagey fox had stepped right on the trap trigger. He was caught! Tracks in the wild tell their own story.

Stanley asked, "How much do you think a fox hide like that might bring."
"I don't know for sure, but you see rich ladies in the cities wearing fox coats. Suppose as much as twenty-five dollars!"
"Wow! That's a lot of money!"

"How are we going to get him out is the question? He's dug in pretty good."

Stanley said "I'll shoot him in his middle at the edge of the hole, you grab his legs and see if you can pull him out. If that doesn't work maybe you can pull him a little further and I'll shoot him again!" Seemed logical at the time.

Stanley aimed and shot. I grabbed the back legs and pulled. During the heat of the excitement, I didn't think of how all the saplings around the den were chewed off, and consider he might turn, come out of that hole, and bite me right in the face! I'd already been bitten once that day, and once was plenty!

I could feel the fox digging even deeper into the hole with his front legs. He was hard to budge. Stanley then got down in the hole beside me, in bite range, and said, "If you can pull him out just an inch or two further, I'll shoot him again."

I braced my feet against the side of the den hole and pulled with all my might. The fox came out another couple inches, Stanley placed another shot into his middle at the edge of the hole. I pulled again, and the fox gave up another couple inches. Stanley shot again. We did that four or five times, then I could feel the fox relax and he came on out of the den, dead as dead can be!

He was the biggest fox we had ever seen. We had caught him in our skunk trap! Thanks to a rabbit running towards the hole of the skunk den, and two inches of snow that concealed the trap. His red coat of fur was breathtakingly beautiful.
"Maybe forty dollars!" Stanley exclaimed.

"Maybe! Grab the other hind leg and let's take him to town."

To a little town of a total population five hundred and seventy-seven, two ten-year-old boys walking into town toting the biggest red fox any of them had ever seen, caused quite a stir. Stanley and I, and the fox, were the big news of the day. We proudly paraded the fox down the front sidewalk of main street, pausing at each storefront window as we went. Milking the crowd for all it was worth. Patrons coming out of the stores would gather and make comments. Praise was welcomed. Recognition for ten-year-old boys is hard to come by. The drug store owner, who had sold one piece of chocolate candy every evening to Miss Ruby, came out to see what everyone was looking at. Looking the Fox over he asked, "Where did you catch that big critter anyway?" We told him where and of course added how this savage beast had torn up the ground and all the trees around trying to escape from the trap. The feed store manager, city barber, butcher and shop owners all came out for a look. As they admired the beauty of the red fox, they asked us how on earth we had managed to accomplish such a feat.

We smiled and remained silent and simply basked in the warm glow of boyhood heroism. Of course, there was no reason to mention the rabbit and the two inches of freshly fallen snow had been the real reason for the catch. Silence has golden returns. We told the story of the episode over and over to main street shoppers coming in for their weekly supplies. Several farmers congratulated us for catching it. Said they had lost a good many chickens to a big red fox that had been raiding their chicken house and figured this one could be the culprit. Several patted us on the shoulder and said, "Good job!" By late afternoon the traffic had slowed considerably, and my mother had sent word for me to get on home for supper. Stanley drug the fox into their nearby family store where I think his father skinned it and sold the hide. Fame is great, but somewhat fleeting. I often wondered what lady in which city might have worn that fox fur, draped around her neck as a fur scarf, or part of a coat. Hope she was a pretty lady, as it was a pretty fox!

To this day, when I'm in some fine store that sells ladies' fur coats. My eye drifts over to the section where fox fur is displayed. Walking over for a closer look, I run my fingers through the fur, and am reminded of the day of glory, realized by Stanley and me. Two great trappers from the planes of Missouri, who were blessed with a lucky catch!

Dear reader this is not the end of the story about a fox!

FOX II

It was a year later. The autumn weather was the pleasant kind they call an Indian Summer which is warm and fells more like summer than fall. Stanly and I needed some hunting action, so we decided to grab our guns and go quail hunting north of town.

We had to walk a couple miles before we got into hunting territory. Never mind the distance, the weather was great, trees were dressed in their fall finery of red and gold, and we were young and enjoyed every step. As soon as we stepped to the edge of the destined field, a covey of quail got up. The flutter of their wings is loud, always startles you, and gets your heart pumping like crazy. They were too far off for a good shot. We fired anyway hoping for a lucky kill. Wild quail, unlike the mushy ones, served in restaurants, even high-end restaurants, are a flat-out delicacy. The wild taste is much better. Our mothers were always highly pleased when we brought home quail for the dinner table.

We walked on a few yards further. We noticed the covey had veered off into the timber, where they would be much harder to hunt. While pondering whether to go in the timber after them, Stanley whispered under his breath "Fox!"

Sure enough, straight ahead was a grey fox laying down at the edge of the field. We simultaneously raised our guns and fired at the same time, but the fox didn't move. Apparently, we had killed him stone dead. Running up to review the trophy quarry we had just shot, we noticed there was not a drop of blood to be seen. That was odd. Then Stanley grabbed one of its hind feet and pulled. The fox was stiff.

There was a reason for no blood, it had apparently been dead for several days and was stiff as a board. Crestfallen, we decided to walk into the timber a few yards to see if we could kick up a few quail. No luck.

We then circled back around and found ourselves back staring at the fox again. Lying there as still as a rock. It was obvious this grey fox wasn't nearly as pretty as the red fox we had trapped last year. Nevertheless, we had shot it hadn't we, and it was a fox! Remembering the glory of last fall, and thirsting for more boyhood recognition, we decided to take it to town and say we had shot it, which we indeed had. Sort of! Remaining silent of course about the fact it was dead beforehand, and we had found it lying in the field, was a fact we chose to omit.

Upon returning to town we were quite thirsty and decided to go into Stanley's dad's store for a bottle of pop, before dragging our prize up and down Main Street in search of more boyhood recognition and admiration. The red fox had been such a glorious success, a repeat performance would be most desirable indeed! Stanley's big brother Jimmy was minding the store.

JIMMIE

Jimmie was several years older than Stanley and me. Tall, blue eyed, fair-haired, and movie star handsome. Plus, he was a great fighter and could lick any guy in the county. That was one complete package. I didn't have a big brother. To say I admired him was to put it mildly. I mentally adopted him for my big brother, whether he knew about it or not! Hero worship.

He was sitting in a chair beside the stove as we came in and plopped the grey fox down in front of him. Stanley went over and opened a coke, I popped the top of a tall orange, and we sat down on a bench near Jimmie.

"Where'd you boys get that fox?" asked Jimmie.

"Out on the Taylor farm. Little over two miles from here," Stanley replied.

"Not near as pretty as the red fox you two brought in last year about this time."

"No, it's not!" I piped in. "But it's still a fox!"

"Yes, it is," he said. "I can see that. Did you shoot it?"

"Yes, we did!" We chimed in.

"What do you mean, we?"

138

"We saw the fox lying there asleep in the field and we both shot at the same time! Killed him stone dead!"

"Did he kick or anything after you shot?" he asked.

"Never moved a muscle," we answered in unison.

"I imagine that's about right." He leaned over from his chair and said, "Did you notice there wasn't a drop of blood on him anywhere?"

We said we'd noticed that.

"There's usually a little blood showing, especially if it was shot by two people!"

About that time Stanley developed an itch under his shirt collar.

"And another thing," Jimmie went on to say, "did you notice it's eyes? Both of you bend over here and take a closer look at his eyes."

We bent over, heads nearly touching, looking down into the eyes of the dead fox.

"Did you notice they're all dried out?"

I hadn't taken off my jacket when I came in and I was suddenly getting quite warm.

Jimmie continued, "I've hunted all my life, shot about every wild varmint there is around here to hunt, and I've never seen a varmints eyes dry out the very minute it's shot! Usually takes a week or so for that to happen. Plus, it's stiff as a board. Would you think a fox that had just been shot would have time to get stiff that quick and not show a drop of blood, and have its eyes all dried out?"

We both just looked down and said nothing.

"You boys aren't telling the truth, are you? Every man in this town hunts. Did you two think you could just walk in here, and get by showing this old stiff, dried out eyed dead fox you found out in a field somewhere, saying you had just shot it, and anybody would believe you?"

Creditability once lost, is hard to regain.

Leaning back in his chair, he said, "Now listen boys. If you ever hope to grow up and amount to anything in this life, you can't go around trying to deceive people like you were thinking about doing just now, with this fox story you cooked up."

We dropped our heads in regret. We'd been found out! It especially hurt since Jimmie was everything I wasn't.

"Stanley you go on home for supper and Bennie you go home to your mother too and I'll take this old dead fox you found out in the country somewhere and get rid of it. Just don't let me hear of you two trying anything like that again!"

Our beloved Jimmie has long since passed away. Living far off at the time, I wasn't made aware of his earthly departure, until months later. I felt bad that I hadn't been able to attend his funeral. What you don't know, you don't know.

Years later while driving through our little town where we grew up, I remembered that they had brought Jimmie back there to be buried. The once pristine little town was in terrible need of repair. The brick on the building where his dad had their grocery store had crumbled and fell down in the back. A few doors down, Mom's restaurant was now a store house for odds and ends. I looked through the window. The ceiling, which was made of unusual, decorated metal squares still hung in place. I remembered them well. The brick in the rear of the restaurant had also fallen. It then occurred to me I should drive out to the cemetery and see if I could find Jimmie's grave. Remembering it was only two miles away, I drove west and pulled through the cemetery gates five minutes later.

As I drove up and down the cemetery roads, I recognized the names of many people I had known so well as a boy. Seeing their names, chiseled into the grey tombstones, filled me with a sense of melancholy. I could recall their faces, and their memories came back to me one by one, as I drove slowly by. I still missed them! Rounding the corner of the cemetery road, right in front of me, I saw Jimmie's grave.

For some reason my memory flashed back to the evening when Stanley and I watched Jimmie getting dressed up to go out on a big boy date. Big stuff to us! He had shaved, splashed a touch of after-shave on his face, and put on a white shirt. I asked why he didn't put on an undershirt beneath his white shirt, which was customary in those days, as it was a cool night. He smiled and looked at me and said, "So I can get closer to the girl!" Funny, how you sometimes remember the strangest things, at the oddest times.

Turning off the car's ignition, I stepped out onto the cemetery road. It was early spring, but the air felt and smelled like it was still winter. I pulled my light jacket out of the back seat, zipped it up, and slowly walked up to Jimmie's grave. It seemed surreal, seeing his name carved on a tombstone. Jimmie, with his blonde hair, blue eyes, and statuesque physique, reminded me of paintings I'd seen of the Arch Angel Michael. Men like that just shouldn't die! But Jimmy did!

I knelt on my right knee, feeling the chilly ground through the fabric of my pants, still damp and cold from the rain, and began saying a prayer for Jimmie's soul. I recalled Jimmy giving Stanley and me a growing up lesson to think about, without our knowing what he was doing. Being handsome and all that, he once said

"When you're older and have some experiences
dating girls, after you get home, look in the mirror and
ask yourself, 'Am I winning, or am I losing?' Don't
ever lose your way!"

141

I then heard a bird calling from high overhead. Looking up I saw a smallish white bird, circling and circling. It looked like a small seabird, but no sea birds would have been this far north. In all my years of living here, I had never seen a white bird like that. I lingered there with my memories of Jimmie a while longer. I had never had a chance to tell Jimmie goodbye. I recalled fondly my childhood and his kindness. He was Stanley and my protector, and corrector, when we got a little bit too rowdy, or strayed a bit far from the truth. I needed to thank him for that. The bird didn't leave. It kept calling and circling and circling and calling high overhead. It then occurred to me that Jimmie would do a thing like that, to say goodbye to me, if he could. I stood up, brushed off my right knee, and saluted the bird or Jimmie's spirit, whichever it was. Walking back to the car, I felt a sense of relief. I'd finally had the chance to come back home and thank Jimmie for being my friend, and to say a proper goodbye. A man sometimes must do a thing like that. He would have done the same for me.

I go to church regularly, have listened to numerous fine sermons, and been in an audience blessed by two Popes in Rome. However, when I tell my grandchildren bedtime stories, and the importance of telling the truth, it's Jimmie's reference to the fox, with the dried-out eyes, that I tell them about. The proverb says, "A lying tongue is its owner's enemy." The "talking too" Jimmie gave Stanley and me about always telling the truth at an early age, has served us long and well. Thank you, Jimmie!

SETTLING A SCORE!

While having coffee around the kitchen table one morning, my Dad and his friend Billy Jim commented on how weak American beer was and what they would really like was a good German beer. A stout bock! They decided to try and brew some on their own and ordered "those good German kind of ingredients" they had read about from a catalogue that sold instructions on how to brew German beer. Mom had put an old wood cook stove she didn't need out in the corner of the back yard. It rested in the cool shade of a mulberry tree.

She stored canned tomatoes there. It wasn't canning season yet, so they decided the cook stove would be a perfect place to store and mellow German bock beer. They sent away for brown bottles and bottle caps. After they had brewed fifty bottles or so, they deposited their European style creation within the stove, closed the oven door and waited. According to the catalogue, it could take a few days' time for it to properly mellow. Kept of course in a controlled temperature environment. The old wood stove under the mulberry tree should be just the thing.

After a few days of mellowing, the early August temperature taking an unexpected turn, raised to a hundred degrees, uncommon for that part of the country. Mom woke up suddenly around midnight and shouted,

"Someone's shooting a shotgun in the back yard! Two shots!" Dad jumped up, grabbed his shotgun, pumped a shell in the magazine and with flashlight in hand, stepped off the porch. Gun at the ready, searching the backyard from front to back with his light, no culprit could be seen. He looked most irritated!

With me standing right behind him, another shot went off. Dad and I both flinched. Then we caught the whiff of beer. That good German kind, with quality ingredients, that under certain conditions, turned out to be most explosive. Dad, flashlight in hand, approached and cautiously opened the stove's oven door. Where three bottles of beer had once stood, chards of glass and beer covered the other forty-seven bottles.

With extreme haste Dad shut the oven door and said, "Go to the house!" I took off at a quick pace and he wasn't far behind. The shade of the mulberry tree hadn't kept the beer cool enough. There were forty-seven bottles of liquid dynamite left in Mom's old cook stove, with quality ingredients of the German kind, ready to blow at any minute. Five more blew during the night. Mother was not pleased. Turning to me she said, "Never open that door! The bottles could explode at any time and the pieces of glass could blind you."

The next morning, my friend Beverly came over. The only boy I have ever known by that name. We thought we might go fishing and decided to dig some fishing worms out by the barn. There was a dandy little pond full of perch and blue gill nearby, just a half mile away, and our mothers always welcomed a good stringer of fish. With meat so hard to come by, fish was a mealtime treat, plus they were great fun to catch.

I told Bev about last night's explosions. Curiosity being always at the zenith with young boys, he asked if I would open the stove door just a bit, so he could peek in and see this threat firsthand. Just a little peek wouldn't hurt! I said I was told not to do that, but excitement is hard to come by in small rural town and Bev was my friend. We approached the wood stove, under the mulberry tree, with great caution. I was reaching to open the oven door handle when Beverly hissed under his breath, "The Zarker dog!"

I looked up and walking through my Dad's open barn door, going inside to have a look around, never noticing Bev and I digging worms nearby, was the town's most proficient kid-biter of all time, the Zarker dog!

Opportunity knocked! Without a second thought or an ounce of fear, I ran towards the barn door as fast as I could, slammed it shut, and dropped the iron latch bar in place so there was no escaping! It was a half door. Beverly and I could see over the top. The mean eyed dog, with fangs bared, charged the door, wanting to sink those teeth into us if he possibly could! He tried but couldn't jump that high! We were out of his reach!

Exchanging knowing glances, Bev said, "I'll run home and call the guys!"

In our tiny town with a population of five hundred seventy-seven, kids knew the name of every cat and dog in the entire town. Zarker dog was all that needed to be said.

"I'll tell them to bring clods and rocks," he said.

To which I added, "Sticks too! And let them know we've got him trapped!"

The day of evening-up the score had arrived!

In the 1940's, during and right after World War II, winning was not just the thing, it was the only thing if you wanted to survive. If someone attacked your country, you attacked back. Same way with kids back then, you were taught to fight back! Even-up the score and win, if you could! Even when you fought a bully and couldn't win, you made the point!

I had gathered a small pile of clods, a few pebbles, and a good throwing stick or two from the barnyard, and comfortably leaned over the half gate and eyed my nemesis. My mind ran back to the lovely snow-covered morning, riding on my sled, delightfully being pulled by my Dad around our little town, smiling and waving at neighbors as we passed by. Then having this mean eyed Zarker dog, fangs bared, bearing down on me as my pull rope played out. I recalled a flashback moment of fear as he bore down on me, running silently through the snow, and then feeling his vicious bite, in the middle of my back.

The desire for revenge welled up in my chest as Bev and I looked over top of the half door at the fanged menace, walking back and forth half way across the barn floor, growling at us, making evident his desire to sink his teeth into our hide wherever and whenever he could.

Both Tommy and Jackie came within minutes. They each had a sack of handpicked projectiles for the battle. The four of us stuck our heads over the half barn door, quickly stepping back when the Zarker dog lunged at us, and nearly reaching the top of the half door.

Nothing else was said, we knew it was time, and each boy reached for whatever he had gathered to throw. It was time to avenge the bitten! In Jackie's sack were green pears hard as a rock, picked from his mother's tree. When the dog turned broadside, Jackie wound up and threw everything he had behind his left-handed pitch. He hit the dog dead center in the ribs. The dog, completely enraged at the audacity of boys, who always ran whenever they saw him coming, bared his fangs and ran towards the door, jumped as high as he could again, but couldn't reach us. He bit at the wood on the door.

With that, all four boys let loose with a torrent of cuss words we weren't supposed to know, threw sticks, stones, more green pears and anything else we could find laying in the barnyard.

After being hit a couple dozen times with whatever was handy to throw, he backed up next to the back wall and defiantly glared at us. His mean eyes told us if he could get at us, we would pay dearly. The last thing we could possibly throw was gleaned from the barnyard.

Then my eye caught the steel trap that Dad had hung on a nail on the side of the barn. The lucky trap! The one that caught the big red fox!

As I walked over to lift the trap off the nail, my thoughts drifted back to the plume of the fox's beautiful red tail, sticking straight up in the air, with the blanket of pristine white snow contrasting in the background. With that picture still in my mind, I reached for the chain and lifted my trap off the nail.

The other boys stood back. I started slowly swinging the trap around my head. Two feet of chain allowed a hefty amount of momentum to build. I wondered for a moment what David felt like while whirling his sling shot around his head. Goliath was one scary opponent! So was the Zarker dog. I got all the momentum I could possibly get from swinging the trap in a circle, looked the dreaded Zarker dog right in his mean eyes, and let the trap fly.

There must have been a bit of magic in that old trap. It flew straight as an arrow towards the Zarker dog and hit him square in the nose.

A cheer went up from the boys, as the Zarker dog dropped to his knees. Like all bullies when confronted and beaten, he cowed down and crawled towards the door. He wanted out! The four of us exchanged glances, nodded in mutual agreement, stood back a step or two, and unlatched the door. The Zarker dog ran out and off as fast as his legs could carry him, and never looked back.

I never saw that dog again. We had met the enemy and beaten him. I still remember however, the feeling of running out of pull rope behind my Dad's car, on a beautiful snow-white morning, and turning to my right and seeing his fangs bared, about to deliver me the inevitable bite. Wonder if that's the way it will be when my earthly time comes to an end? I hope the final bite is merciful.

THE LUCKY TRAP

It was just four weeks before Christmas. A good two inches of unvarnished snow covered the ground. You could see your breath in the air while walking down the tracks. The same tracks a little further up that Miss Ruby had walked on.

The cold of the winter is a good time for rabbit hunting. Mom said "If you'll go hunting and get a rabbit, I'll hang it out tonight and we'll have it for dinner tomorrow." She had on a pretty blue flowered apron she'd made from a flour sack. For those who are not accustomed to hunting rabbits, you bring home a rabbit, you skin it, dress it for the kitchen where its washed clean and finally hang it out all night in the cold. In the morning it's frozen hard as a board. However, when it's thawed out, the flavor is enhanced, and it becomes quite a nice meal. It was not until many years later, when I was a guest of the Italian government, did I see whole baked rabbits, sharing the same tray cart in a high-end restaurant with pheasants, duck, and quail, did I realize that Mom was right. Rabbits make a very nice meal. I wondered if the chefs froze them first.

I had my reliable 410-gauge shotgun, previously my grandfathers, and if I say so myself, I was a crack shot for a kid of ten years old. Once we were out of town, I started looking along each side of the embankments for rabbit signs. Meaning rabbit tracks in the snow. Not seeing any, the railroad track eventually crossed a small stream and I was surprised to see several muskrats swimming in the tiny stream below.

Just across the stream, rabbit tracks could be seen everywhere. I had the blue color Peters High Performance shell in my gun. It's a good thing it would reach out further than any other shell I'd used. A rabbit burst out of the embankment on my right and was running like the dickens as fast as it could. Not having much time to shoot I hurriedly drew a bead, pulled the trigger, and meat for the table was on the menu for tomorrow.

Carrying the rabbit in one hand and my gun in the other, I stepped between the rail ties and crossed the small creek again. Muskrats were swimming all over the place. I could see the entrance to their den on the east embankment.

Mom was delighted when I came home. The rabbit was dressed and hung outside all night on a string. The next day, rabbit, biscuits and gravy made a fine dinner.

Virtually all rural boys my age wore Levi Strauss jeans. Mine were a little tight and very well worn. Had a hole in one knee. I asked Mom if I could have a new pair for Christmas. She said, we don't have the extra three dollars this year for new jeans. I'll sew yours up tonight and they'll do just fine.

The next day, I saw an older gentleman who did some trapping and I asked him, "How much are fur buyers paying for muskrat hides?"

"Three dollars. You need to skin'em out, stretch them good and tight over a board and dry the hide good. You do know how to do that don't you?"

"Yes, Sir".
I'd seen Papaw do that.

I went back to the barn and pulled the lucky trap off the nail. It had caught the red fox. Smacked the dreaded Zarker dog in the nose, and now maybe it could help me get a pair of new Levi's. I cut a stake, found some wire, and headed out to the little stream under the railroad track. Spotting the entrance to the den, I waded out into the water. It wasn't deep. I tied the end of the trap chain to the wire, wrapped the wire around the wooden stake, and pushed the stake deep in the mud to hold it in place. If I caught a muskrat. After setting the trap right in front of the den entrance, I headed back home. Hoping Momma wouldn't notice my wet pants.

I couldn't wait for school to be over. I dropped my books off at the house and took off for the little creek. When I got there my trap was gone! Had someone stolen it! Then I thought, I might as well reach out into the water to see if I can feel the trap chain just in case it wasn't stolen. With great trepidation I reached down in the water. What if the muskrat was caught and very much alive! He could bite my finger off! I found the trap chain under the water. Pulling slowly, it revealed I had caught a muskrat. I shook it loose from the trap, reset it again, and scurried off for home.

The next afternoon I had caught another one. They say that third time's a charm; on the third day no trap was to be found. I felt around under water. It was gone. Either something like a bear had gotten into it and pulled it away, or the lucky trap had been stolen. Since there were no bears in our county, what had happened was obvious.

I sold each hide for three dollars apiece, took the money and walked straight into Sears and Roebuck and purchased two new pairs of Levi's. I had bought my own clothes! That was a good feeling! The lucky trap had done its duty once again! It would be justified if whoever stole the trap, got his finger pinched a time or two. I suspected who took it but did not care. I never trapped again.

BACK TO STANLEY & ME

CLOTHES LINED!

Halloween is a magical night. Mothers dress up their kids in costume of various characters. That night my mom dressed me up as a monkey. I didn't like it much, but she had made it, and I had to wear it anyway.

I was wearing a black mask. Mom sewed me a well fitted black body suit and meticulously fabricated a long black tail. How she did that I cannot recall. One girl I knew came up to me and said, "Who are you?" I didn't answer as she would recognize my voice, plus the mask made it hard to speak. She never did figure out who I was, so I guess my costume was great after all!

The tail came in handy later in the next spring. Mom had gone out to the hen house to gather the eggs. I remembered the long black tail was still in the corner of my closet. Since entertainment was scant, and knowing Mom was deathly afraid of snakes, I thought it might be a fun trick to retrieve the tail and lay it on the floor of the porch when she was reentering the house. The tail was splendidly sown. I could see her starting to bring the eggs back into the house so I hid in the shadow and placed the tail right where she would step when she walked in. To increase the theatrical effect, I wiggled it about as well. The plan worked perfectly! She saw the tail, screamed bloody murder and threw the egg bucket with eggs up to the ceiling, breaking all the eggs when landing back on the floor. I laughed only a short moment, as she soundly grabbed me by the ear, boxed my ears, made me clean up the broken eggs, and then sent me straight to bed. I learned quickly of course that which is highly entertaining to some, might not be regarded in the same light by others.

Trick or treat were two wondrous words that brought forward dreams of candy, caramel apples, popcorn balls, and sometimes fresh baked doughnuts, still warm from the oven. Small town love!

By eight o'clock, the smaller children had gone home to loving arms that review all the treats they've received. Older boys, of ten or so, yearn for additional excitement. Upon reviewing, and consuming, much of the bounty we had collected, Stanley looked in his bag and said, "Anybody get an apple? An apple might take away some this sugar taste in my mouth from eating all this candy!"

None of us had an apple.

Jackie piped up and said, "Marshall Cooper has a tree that's loaded with apples!"

"The Marshall!" exclaimed Stanley

"Why if we get caught filching an apple from his tree, he might send all of us to the boys' reform school!" I worriedly stated.

The boys' reform school was a threat showered on all mischievous boys. Although no one we knew had ever been sent there, just the thought of being sent to a boy's prison was enough to send the fear of God pulsing through our veins.

"Naw…" said reassuring Jackie. "He's got a whole tree full and would never even miss four little ole' apples! Besides, it's dark and he would never see us anyway!"

Hunger for excitement preceded our hunger for an apple. The four troubadours, ready for adventure, made way for the residence of the good Marshall Cooper!

The kitchen light was on and the open screened window gave us the advantage of both sound and visibility. We heard voices as we approached. Apparently, Marshall Cooper and his wife Edith were just finishing supper. His wife, Edith had a slight speaking impediment and her voice could be easily identified.

"George, did you like the pork chops tonight?"

"Loved'em Edith. How did you come up with that great flavor? Tasted wonderful!"

"Rolled them in cracker crumbs and egg whites, and baked'em. Glad you liked them, you old tin badge you!"

Hearing they had such a good relationship, I started feeling reluctant about our adventure and thought that maybe we ought to go on home. Too late! Jackie had already climbed the tree and was pulling apples off one of the lower limbs. He tossed one to me and I stuffed it in my pocket!

Learned right then and there you can't take back words that've been said, or undo things that've been done! I'd taken one of Marshall and Edith Coopers apples! Maybe she meant it for an apple pie! We shouldn't be doing this!

Looking down, and not feeling so good about myself, I stepped away from the light of the kitchen window. Then I heard George say, "Going out for a smoke Edith!" All four of the Halloween troubadours heard it too!

Then came a whisper spoken in unison, "Run!"

156

It was dark, but I knew which way the road was and ran toward it full tilt. Then a strange thing happened that seemed magical. Something had me by the neck and I was suspended in midair. Maybe witches did come out at Halloween and one had me by the throat! Then I was thrown down on the ground so hard it knocked the breath out of me.

Puzzled as to what had happened, my mind was racing to try and figure the whole thing out when I heard the backdoor slam and footsteps coming in my direction. The Marshall was coming straight towards me! I did my best not to breathe. My heart was pounding so loud it seemed it could have been heard clear uptown. The footsteps stopped just inches from my head. If Marshall Cooper found me, I would without the slightest doubt be sent off to reform school for bad boys. Some hidden force had lifted me up in the air and threw me at his feet, as a reminder it's better to be good! What was it that had grabbed a hold of me and threw me on the ground? An apple from his tree, in my right trouser pocket was irrefutable evidence that I was guilty. Caught! Red apple handed! It looked bad for me! I was full of remorse. I would probably be sent off to the reform school and never see my Mom or Dad, or my little dog Frisky, ever again. I was one of the saddest boys in the world.

I could hear the ritual of lighting a cigarette being performed just above my head. The pack was taken from his shirt pocket. He tapped the pack against his other hand, so a single cigarette would come out, placed it between his lips, and opened the top of the cigarette lighter. A click and flame from the lighter came out, so bright it seemed it would light up the whole yard. The cigarette was lit. Surely, he would see me lying right down by his right foot! He didn't see me! Nothing was said. I didn't breathe! The Marshall then took a deep breath, paused a second, then blew out a puff of smoke. The kitchen window provided just enough light to where I could witness the curling blue smoke, settle right down

Benn Wasson

just beneath my nose. I prayed, please don't sneeze! Nose please doesn't sneeze! I held it! If he moved just one step to his right, he would step on my head. Scaring him to death! Then he would be twice as mad! I couldn't be in a worse predicament!

Then a voice, seeming to come straight from heaven, called out, "George you better come on in!"

"Just a minute honey." Marshall Cooper took a final deep draw.

I was never so aware until at that time, how much the burning ember from a cigarette could light up the night. Please don't look down! He didn't. I heard footsteps walking away. Then the back-screen door slammed shut. I stood up and finally breathed. I hit my head on something when I rose up! Running my hand over the object it felt like a pole. Running my fingers on up, I then realized what had happened. Mrs. Cooper always hung her sheets out to dry on a line, so they would be snow white and smell good! I had run into Mrs. Cooper's clothesline and had been clothes lined! The moral of the story is, if you know something, you're thinking about doing is wrong, then don't do it, or else you too just might get clothes lined!

158

THE MIDNIGHT STAMPEDE

Adventure is always on the mind of small boys. One warm sunny morning in June, Stanley said, "Let's go fishing!"

"Where?" I replied.

"Lick Crick"!

"Why that's ten miles from here! We can't walk that far."

"Bet we could get somebody to take us!"

"Take us?" I replied, "Both our Dads are working, and neither one of our Moms has a car, or can drive, even if they had one! Who could we ask?"

"How about your Granddad and that little red pickup truck he drives? He would take us, wouldn't he?"

"I don't know, guess I could ask him."

"We could stay all night, and he wouldn't have to come back and get us until the next day!"

"You mean sleep there all night?"

"Sure," he said. "We're both ten now and should be no problem at all."

It was starting to sound very thrilling and adventurous.

"I'll have to go and ask my Mom!"

We had stayed all night fishing on the river with our Dads many times, but never by ourselves.

"Mom can I go out to Lick Creek and stay all night fishing with Stanley?"

"What! Absolutely not! You're too young!"

Taking a touch of liberty with the yet unknown from Stanley's side I explained, "Stanley's Mom said it was all right with her, if it was all right with you!"

Pausing for a long minute, she frowned and said, "You would have to cook yourself some supper and then breakfast the next morning! Can you do that?"

"Sure, no problem all. I've watched Dad fry bacon and eggs over the campfire a dozen times."

The only thing our Dads ever cooked when out fishing all night was bacon and eggs in the evening and bacon and eggs for breakfast. Occasionally a can of pork'n beans would be opened turning the evening meal into a gourmet occasion!

"Cooking's no problem Mom!"

Stanley, telling the same story to his mother, received the green light, and it was time for me to approach my grandfather. I didn't know him that well! He and my Grandma, Bessie, Dad's Mom, had divorced years ago, and we didn't visit him much.

I saw the little red truck sitting in front of his house, realizing he was home I walked up and knocked on the door. He had remarried, and his wife answered the door. She was a largish friendly woman with curly hair. I mentioned that Stanley and I wanted to go out to Lick Creek and spend the night fishing and wondered if grandpa might take us. He was just walking into the room as I finished speaking and said "Sure son! I'll pick you up at four o'clock this afternoon."

"Great! Pick us up at Stanley's Dad's store," while running out the door. Wow! We had lots to do in a short period of time.

I found Stanley sweeping the floor of his Dad's grocery store and blurted out, "The fishing trip's on, Grandpa's picking us up at four o'clock."

The clock hand had just turned two!

He said, "I'll box up something for us to eat while you get some fishing line and hooks at the hardware store."

"Deal!"

And off I ran to ask my Mom for some money. Young boys made up their own fishing lines in those days, no one I knew had enough extra money to buy rod and reels.

I bought a roll of fishing line, hooks and sinkers. Stanley always carried a pocketknife we could use to cut the line, and my dad had a hatchet we could use to cut willow saplings to use for poles.

"Stanley!" I exclaimed running into the store, "Bait, we don't have any bait!

"My Dad gave us some liver we can use, but worms are better!"

There's a wet spot behind our barn where you can always find fishing worms. Let's go."

In no time at all we had two large coffee cans full of worms. Mom handed me a blanket and a pillow. "Be careful," she said, looking apprehensive as we scurried off to the store. Feeling full of adventure, I didn't even look back.

At exactly four o'clock the little red pickup truck drove up in front of the grocery store and Stanley and I piled in the back, and off we went. In about fifteen minutes the land of opportunity sprang into view. A small bridge crossed Lick Creek. A narrow stream, lined with trees, was surrounded by lush grassland on both sides. It was a beautiful spot as groomed as a golf course. Grandpa drove across the bridge. We eagerly grabbed our supplies and headed for the fence. Cattle obviously grazed the pastures.

"Pick you up at nine o'clock in the morning."

"Ok!" we said, as I was handing Stanley the grocery box over the fence. The truck pulled away, leaving a trail of dust blowing in the wind.

We looked at each other and said, "We made it! We're out here all by ourselves, and no one to tell us what to do!" This was freedom!

We started for the creek with a happy step. A large tree, not far from the fence, with branches that spread out, covered an area offering an ideal spot to make camp. As luck would have it, right near the big tree, was an old tree stump, cut long ago, whose curved roots stood out about a foot above ground, forming the perfect place to set a frying pan! We sat our grocery box and supplies down right on top of the old stump. "Handy!"

Stanley said, "Why don't you take the hatchet and cut us some bank poles and I'll cut some lines and put hooks on them."

I headed for a group of small willows beside the creek and started chopping. The saplings were tougher than I thought, and it took several whacks to get each one cut. I wore a blister on my hand but finished and gathered up the poles and dropped them on the ground back at camp. We promptly tied the lines on the poles, baited the hooks and stuck them firmly in the ground at creeks edge. Stanley had placed the big frying pan on the stumps curved root and was opening the package of bacon.

"Why don't you find some dried sticks to put under the pan and we'll start supper!

"Won't take long," I said gathering small sticks to put on the bottom of the pile with larger one's on top.

"Perfect."

Pulling out a match, striking it on his hexagon rifle barrel he had brought along, lit the small sticks on the bottom which quickly blossomed into a flame, setting the bigger sticks on fire, heating up the big iron skillet and we were ready to start cooking bacon.

Bacon and eggs, three each, bread, and a bottle of soda pop went down easily, between expressed hopes of what we might find on our poles in the morning. The sun was starting to set. We sat the frying pan aside and started gathering bigger pieces of wood to burn through the night.

The fire was soon giving off a bright light as we unrolled our blankets and placed our pillows under a spot where we could see through the tree's branches and look at stars in the sky.

"Wonder what's up there," surmised Stanley.

"I don't know."

"Think there's anybody up there looking down at us?"

About then a star went racing across the sky.

"I hear if you see a falling star and make a wish, your wish will come true," I volunteered.

"I've heard that too."

The fire was dying down, crickets were chirping, and our eyelids became heavy and we dropped off into a peaceful childhood sleep.

I suddenly heard thunder, and sat up abruptly and thought, gee I didn't think it was going to rain. The fire had gone out, everything was pitch black and I couldn't see a thing! However, it wasn't going to rain, and it wasn't thunder. It was the sound of the hooves of stampeding cattle! Seconds later a herd of black angus cattle, was running full tilt through our camp and bawling at the top of their lungs. I shouted, 'Stampede!" Anyone of them could have knocked us down and trampled us to death.

Dust filled the air! It was hard to breathe! Bawling cattle, up close, makes a loud and frightening sound! Especially if you're small and they're big! Some were running by me so close I could smell their sweat. I was beyond scared, totally terrified! "Stanley" I shouted hoping he could hear me above the din of the bawling cattle and thundering hoofs. No answer. Oh God, I thought to myself, what if cattle ran over him and he's dead and I'm out here all alone! One of the cattle kicked the frying pan. The noise made the cattle run even faster and bawl even louder.

Suddenly, I remembered the direction of the fence. It was only a few yards from our camp and if I could make it over to the fence, I would be safe. I strained to see the cattle when they were coming my way. I could hear their hoofs pounding down on the ground. But there was no moon, it was a dark night, and the cattle were pitch black. I couldn't see anything!

I made a plan. Wait until the sound of hoof beats passed by, hope the coast was clear, then make a mad dash for the fence. A large group, circling the camp, passed by, then I ran for the fence as fast as my feet could carry me! A flood of relief washed over me when my hand touched the fence wire. All I had to do was climb the fence and get on the other side, and I would be safe! Grabbing the top strand of wire, I started climbing as fast as I could. My hands and legs were shaking but I kept climbing! I swung my right leg over the top strand thinking, I'll be safe! But complete terror had taken its toll, and for some reason, beyond my comprehension, I could not lift my left leg to get over the fence! I was paralyzed with fear! Frozen in place, completely unresponsive. I tried to lift my leg again. I couldn't! The frightening thought of falling back on the cattle side and being trampled to death encouraged me to try with all my might once again to lift my left leg. Might as well have weighed a ton.

I couldn't believe this was happening! It was surreal! Then the thought of gravity came to mind. If I could lean my body far enough to the right, gravity would tip me over to fall on the safe side of the fence. I would be saved! The top strand was barbed wire! If my left leg got caught in one of the sharp barbs it would be torn badly. Plus, my jeans would be torn, and Mom would be mad. But fear of being trampled to death made the decision easy for me, I leaned over to the right as far as I could, gravity indeed took hold, and I went tumbling to the ground. Safe! A flood of relief swept over me like drops from a warm summer rain. No torn leg, or pants and safe!

Am I alone out here? "Stanley!" I shouted over the sound of pounding hooves and that incessant sound of bawling.

I heard a faint voice say, "Over here! I'm up in the big tree!"

"O.K., I'm on the roadside of the fence. Did you bring a flashlight?" I shouted.

"Stuck it in my back pocket just before I climbed the tree!" He flickered it a few times in my direction.

"Wow! That's great! I'll come back over the fence once they leave."

After what seemed an eternity they finally left. It was eerily quiet. I called out, "Stanley are you o.k.?"

"Yes!"

"Wonder what caused those cattle to act like that?"

"I don't know but they were scared to death by something that's for sure!"

I climbed back over the fence; my left leg worked again. Stanley had his flashlight out surveying the damage. Tomorrow morning's eggs had been stepped on were history, the bacon had been stepped on too, but the package hadn't ripped open and was still edible. The blankets where we had been sleeping on were trampled into the dust, as we would have been, if we hadn't run for safety.

Stanley said, "Come over here and stand next to me." With that he raised his hexagon-barreled rifle and started shooting in the darkness in a complete circle all around us. Nothing else bothered us further throughout the night.

Not much can damage an iron skillet, so the next morning, bacon was the sole offering on the breakfast menu. Pulling up our fishing lines revealed we didn't catch a thing. Guess the fish were scared too.

We rolled up our blankets, tossed the skillet over the fence, and sat down on the safe side of the fence, not saying much to each other. Finally, Stanley said, "Wonder if I might have shot a cow?"
"Didn't see any laying around, so I guess not!"
With that the little red truck came into view and with great relief we hopped into the back of the truck. Our all-night Lick Creek adventure was over. It was an episode never to be forgotten!

AFTERTHOUGHT

At the age of ten, I was puzzled at what it could have been that caused a large herd of black angus cattle to go completely berserk, bawling at the top of their lungs, and stampede madly through our little camp. There were no bears, mountain lions, wolves, or any large predator that could have inspired that kind of fright. Then in later years, I remembered another strange happening. An event you might say.

At the age of seven or eight, we were living on the farm, and Momma didn't have enough eggs to bake a cake. Our hens had stopped laying. Dad was at work, and he had the only family car. Besides, Mom couldn't drive anyway. When we moved to the farm, we found a large population of wild guinea fowl that roosted in the tall trees just behind our hen house. Round bodied, speckled black and white with white heads, bright red combs, making a clipped clucking sound, resembled something appearing like a clown in a circus. They wouldn't nest with the hens but preferred to nest out in the wild in the pasture. Their eggs were smaller than a chicken egg. Guinea shells were tan and sometimes speckled and tasted better! Momma said, "Son, why don't you go out into the pasture and see if you can find a guinea nest and bring back enough eggs so I can finish this cake". She normally wouldn't let me cross the fence as there was a white-faced Hereford bull who lived there that had a bad temper, but her cake needed eggs!

I looked around, didn't see any bull, so out into the pasture I went. Frisky came with me looking for a rabbit she could chase. I walked out in the grassland for a few moments, hadn't found anything, when I suddenly heard a loud sound like roaring coming from behind me. It scared me and Frisky and we started running away from the sound, but I stumbled and fell face down. Looking up to see what was making that noise, I saw huge grey green triangle shaped something flying at a low altitude, right over my head. I'd never seen any flying thing that looked like that. Frisky was scared too and came over and crouched next me. Whatever it was quickly flew away into the distance. Frisky then got up and started sniffing around the pasture.

I heard Momma calling "Found any eggs yet?" I got up looking around to see if that flying thing had come back. Coast was clear. Looking to my left, I saw a large clump of grass. Seemed like a likely place. Sure enough, there was a nest right in front of me. Twenty small light tan eggs, lying in a perfect round circle, were right in the middle of the clump of grass. Frisky went over and gave them a sniff. There were so many I couldn't carry them in my hands. Not wanting to leave this treasure trove, I took off my long-sleeved shirt, tied the sleeves at the cuffs so the eggs wouldn't spill out, tied the top, and proceeded triumphantly back to Mom with twenty guinea eggs. Mom happily baked a nice cake for Dad, which we all enjoyed. She and I had scrambled guinea eggs for lunch.

The year was 1942, and I can't tell you to this day what that triangle flying thing was that flew over my head. Something did! It scared the dickens out of me! Frisky too! Kind of got me wondering again, what it was that so frightened that herd of black angus cattle so much when Stanley and I were camping out on Lick Creek! Didn't seem to make much sense to me. Many years later I did meet Robert and Ed who were in Roswell in 1947, the year they found the crashed flying saucer. They looked me square in the eye and said, "You danged right' the event happened!" Hard to doubt men of that character! After all, the universe is such a big place, who am I to judge?

THE CHRISTMAS MIRACLE

It was Christmas! We were going to Granny and Papaw's house for Christmas Eve to open more presents there the following Christmas Day! Momma, Dad and I exchanged our presents early Christmas Eve morning. I drew each one a picture telling them I loved them. I was not much of an artist. I got a puzzle. I tried not to show my disappointment, knowing money was scarce. They started to pack for the trip. As we were starting for the door, Dad turned to me and said he had forgot his cigarette lighter in their bedroom and asked me to go back and get it for him. He thought it might be under the covers. I ran into their bedroom, I couldn't see it anywhere, then flipped back the blanket to look for the lighter and to my complete surprise, there was a brand-new Red Ryder BB gun! I had wished and wished for one but never thought I would ever get one. It was beautiful! There was also a round yellow roll of five hundred BB's. I could shoot five hundred times. I was happy beyond words! Every man in our extended family was a hunter, and I wanted to be a hunter too. This was my best Christmas present ever! I hugged and thanked Dad profusely.

"Think of the consequences before you pull the trigger and you'll get along just fine."

"I sure will Dad!"

I put the gun in the car first thing, so we'd be sure and not forget it. Childhood exuberance and restraint rarely walk hand in hand!

Papaw and Granny had a big rooster that was as onerous as they come. For some reason or the other, Granny had named him Lollipop when he was just a little chick. He grew up, big, mean, and no sweet chicken was he! Lollipop was dark red, with a ring of black feathers that circled his neck. His comb was tall, a bright red, and leaned over on the left side, partially covering his left eye. Made him look like a rooster pirate! His wide-open right eye, mean looking and ominous, focused on me every time I was in the backyard and chased me each time he saw me. I was convinced he hated me! Lollipop was a free-range roaming rooster. That meant he could be everywhere and free to attack me anywhere he could find me! Long spurs on the back of each foot, were perfect for raking the bare legs of small boys on their way to the outdoor toilette. Being the recipient of many such experiences, I knew Lollipop's modus of operandi, and was scared every time I went to the outhouse.

Outdoor toilettes, common in those days were cold in the winter, and hot in the summer and for obvious reasons, were located quite a distance from the house. No rural people we knew of had an indoor bathroom. Lollipop's favorite technique was a sneak attack from the rear. On your way to the outhouse, he would come up, unseen from behind, cackling loudly and flapping his wings, and spurring! Scared me silly! If you fell, he'd jump right on you, raking anywhere he could land a spur. Old Lollipop had sent me back into the house several times sniffling to my mother that old Lollipop had got me.

I gave Granny a hug when we walked in the back door. She was a white haired, petite; blue eyed little lady, with a disposition sweet as honey. She had flour on her cheek, and I could see she was about to put another one of her delicious peach cobblers in the oven. I promptly found Papaw in the living room sitting by the stove. He chewed tobacco and had his usual spit pan nearby. I showed him my new BB gun. He was an outdoor man and avid hunter. He poured some of the BBs from the yellow roll in his hand, and said, "Be careful, these could knock an eye out".

"O.K. Papaw," I said and proceeded to go out into the barnyard.

Papaw had a wooden buckboard wagon. I climbed up on it, imagination at work, and promptly thought it would be a handy place to fight off a band of murderous renegades. Then I saw out in the barnyard, pecking on the ground, the meanest renegade I knew of. The dreaded kid chasing, wing flapping, leg raking, Lollipop!

With the skill and determination of my rifleman, great, great, great, grandfather, John Wasson, who genealogists say fought under General George Washington in the Battle of Brandywine Creek during the Revolutionary War, poured twenty BBs in my hand, filled up the gun, and looked over the side of the buckboard at the murderous villain, Lollipop! The Battle of the Barnyard was on!

Either Papaw or Granny had thrown some shelled corn on the ground and Lollipop was looking ever so content, swallowing corn kernels one by one. One of the lighter colored hens came over to join in, and Lollipop promptly fluffed up his feathers and chased her off. Chivalry around the kitchen table was apparently not a part of his love life.

The buckboard was about five feet off the ground. Giving me a perfect view of the dreaded leg scratcher. When I peeked over the side of the buckboard, he didn't see me. I cocked my BB gun, placing a BB in the chamber, rested my gun on the lip of the buckboard for a good steady aim, placed the front sight on the rear end of Lollipop, lined it up with rear sight, and pulled the trigger. Lollipop clucked, jumped up a foot off the ground, hurriedly turned around in a circle, wings spread out in attack mode, to fight whoever it was that had pecked him in the rear. Nothing was there. Puzzled, he looked around for a minute or two, and then went back to eating corn. This was more fun than a boy was entitled to! I shot a second time, he jumped even higher this time and with wings again spread in a fighting mode looking around to find some chicken to fight. This was glorious! I then shot a third and a fourth time. He jumped up, clucked and spread his wings after each shot. Lollipop wasn't about to give up his corn feast. After each shot, he returned to the business at hand, of eating corn. I was readying to repeat that performance for the fifth time, when Mom called out the kitchen door, "It's time for dinner."

"I'll be right there."

I cocked the gun for one last shot at Lollipop and took aim.

"Dinner's getting cold! Get yourself right on here!"

Glancing at her, I took my eye off Lollipop for a second and pulled the trigger. That very instant, Lollipop abruptly turned around, and the BB, flying straight as an arrow for his rear end, hit him instead squarely in the head. Lollipop dropped like a rock! Stone dead!

I stared in utter disbelief. This can't be happening! It's Christmas Eve! I was just called for dinner, peach cobbler for dessert, and I just shot and killed Lollipop. Granny and Papaw's only rooster! I was in the worst trouble ever! Dad had said, "Think of the consequences before you pull the trigger and you'll get along just fine!" I'd taken my eye off the target when Mom called out the kitchen door, pulled the trigger without thinking of the consequences. I didn't get along just fine! I must be in more trouble than any boy in Ralls County.

Fathers didn't say much back then when a boy misbehaved. They simply grabbed the kid and gave them a good whipping. "I didn't mean

173

to do it" explanations didn't go far. Every man carried a pocketknife in those days. When men folks got together, they would discuss pocketknives, examined each other's' knives, and sometimes traded them with one another. It was the custom. The worst kind of whipping a boy could get was when the father brought out his pocketknife, unfolded the longest blade, and handed the knife to his son. Not a word was necessary. Every boy knew he had seriously crossed the line when that happened, and what was required. You took your Dad's knife, walked outside to the nearest tree, cut off a branch, brought it back inside, handed the branch to your Dad, bent over and received a whipping from the branch you yourself had cut. It was usually a hard whipping! Walking out to the nearest tree, knife in hand, was a solemn march. Knowing what was sure to come made it doubly solemn!

Dad would no doubt take away my new BB gun. It would be a severe whipping for sure. Terrifying. Welts would probably be raised on my backside and hurt for a few days. Sitting down would be painful. I was going to suffer for my sin, and I deserved it!

I walked to the house quietly, trying to become as invisible as possible. Keeping the BB gun down by my side, not wishing to bring up the topic of any gun whatsoever, silently praying no one noticed I even had one. As silent as a mouse I crept to the back of the kitchen and put it in the pantry where Granny stored her canned Alberta peaches. She had several jars in there. Their large Alberta peach tree was a good producer.

At dinner, I sat next to Momma, spoke only when spoken to, determined to be as quiet as possible. I could barely eat. Anything that is, except Grannies peach cobbler with whipped cream on top.

After dinner, Dad sat down with Papaw, as they often did, and told hunting and fishing stories. I loved these stories. Dad loved to hear Papaw tell the story about old Big Mouth, a legendary bass that no one had ever been able to catch.

Old Big Mouth lived in the deepest hole on Spencer Creek. The dark blue water was so deep it was always chilly. One summer, high school boys tried to swim down and touch the bottom. They could never get that deep.

A fisherman who had once hooked old Big Mouth said he broke his cane fishing pole like it was a matchstick. One day, when Papaw was fishing at Spencer Creek, he saw old Big Mouth come to the top of the water and inhale a spring frog that was gliding across the pool. His mouth was so wide it looked like he could swallow a chicken. The word chicken caused me to feel most uncomfortable and full of remorse. I eased back into the kitchen, looked out the window. Lollipop was lying there, still as a stone! I would be known tomorrow as the rooster killer! Papaw and Granny's rooster!

Back in the living room, Papaw was telling about his plan to catch old Big Mouth. He went to New London looking for a big cane pole. A really big one! After going to three stores, he found a great long pole, as thick at the base as a man's wrist. He brought it home, put the strongest fishing line on it he had. The next morning, he got up early, had coffee, bacon and a biscuit sandwich, then started out for the deepest hole on Spencer Creek, looking for Big Mouth! It was mid-August.

Walking along the side of the creek, looking down on the way, he finally saw what he was looking for. Quickly stopping, he bent down and grabbed a big striped spring frog. After once watching Big Mouth devour

175

a big spring frog, Papaw figured it might be one of his favorite meals. As he neared the deep hole, he took off his shoes to walk as softly as possible. Keeping in the shadow of an oak tree, he remained unseen. He did not put a sinker on his line. He wanted the frog to glide across the top of the water, as it would naturally do, like the time he saw Big Mouth swallow one. He hooked the frog on its lip so it could swim freely. Then he raised the big cane pole and tossed the hooked frog out into the middle of the deepest pool in Spencer Creek. Perfectly placed.

The frog just stayed there for a minute or two. Giving a fish below ample time to look it over. The frog then gave a kick and glided about three feet on the surface. It paused a moment or two, and then kicked again. It had just started its second glide when the huge bass rose to the surface and with a huge splash swallowed him in one gulp. Papaw set the hook! The legendary Big Mouth was on the other end of his line!

Old Big Mouth swam a few feet down in the blue depths before he realized he was hooked. Then he turned on the power and bent double Papaw's cane pole, thick as a man's wrist. This was some fighting fish! He took the line down twenty feet or so, pulling half the length of the pole with it. The bass then came to the surface and jumped four feet in the air, savagely shaking his head back and forth trying to throw the hook out. The hook held. Then old Big Mouth took another dive for the bottom, Papaw was holding the pole with both hands. He hoped the fish might be tiring. It was a hot morning and Papaw's shirt was already wringing wet with sweat. Then old Big Mouth took another hard dive, and the cane pole broke in half. He couldn't believe it! That was the stoutest fishing pole he had ever seen and there he was standing there with just half of the pole in his right hand. Old Big Mouth had won again! Disappointed, he stood looking over the pool wondering where the fish had gone, when the other half of his cane pole suddenly floated to the surface. He supposed Big Mouth shook the hook out. Then to his surprise, the remaining half of the pole started moving around. That meant old Big Mouth was still hooked on the other end, and cruising around about twenty feet down, pulling the pole with him as he swam.

Papaw was sixty years old, but a scrapper if there ever was one. He noticed that as Big Mouth swam around in a circle, he would come under a tree branch that was hanging over the water. The sixty-year-old Henry Benn took off his clothes and jumped into the deepest hole in Spencer Creek. It was indeed chilly. Swimming out to the center of the pool, he grabbed the half of his pole that was now claimed by Big Mouth, then swam his way back to the overhanging tree limb, grabbed on with the other hand, and held on for dear life. Feeling the pull of Papaw's hand, Big Mouth, with renewed energy, started fighting again. Diving deep, then powering to the surface and jumping high in the air, shaking his big head back and forth in effort to throw the hook. The hook held again. Papaw desperately hoped the big fish would tire out before he did. The strength of the giant bass was phenomenal. Big Mouth took another hard dive for the bottom. Papaw kept his grip on the pole with one hand and the tree branch with the other. The limber tree branch had a lot of give to it and the fish's pull was so hard it dipped Papaw's head under water. This was incredible! He had never been in a situation like this! This was war! Big Mouth came up and took another dive for the deep, but not quite so deep this time. Papaw got his head above water. The big fish dove and came up again, and again, then after one final run for the deep, he came to the top and rolled over on his side. He was spent! Papaw then pulled the great fish to the side of the pool, ran his hand through the gills of Big Mouth, and lifted him out of the water onto the bank. He had won! He had caught the legendary Big Mouth!

I was so intrigued with the story I momentarily forgot my sorry predicament. I had shot and killed Granny and Papaw's only rooster, Lollipop, and he was lying dead as a door nail out in the barnyard. I would get a whipping tomorrow. Christmas day! Hoping against hope, with the stealth of a shadow, I eased my way again back to the kitchen window. The evening light was fading fast, and Lollipop the terrible, was lying there in his eternal repose, as still as the night. Tomorrow would be a very hard day!

The temperature was dropping. It was going to be a really cold night. The wood stove for the living room was their main heating stove. Granny also burned wood in her kitchen stove, which kept her cooking area warm all day long. Papaw would chuck them both full of wood before going to bed. However, during the night, the fires would go out and sometimes it would get so cold, ice would be formed in Granny's teapot in the morning.

Being that it was so cold, Momma decided it would be best if I slept between Granny and Papaw that night. Their bed covers were thick, heavy, and warm. As sleep began to close boyhood eyes, my heart filled with dread and sadness about the coming morning. They would find out I shot Lollipop! Dad would give me a stern look of disappointment, and without saying a word, take his pocketknife out, open the big blade, hand it to me, and nod towards the door. I knew what I had to do. It was going to be a very unpleasant morning.

Their bedroom faced east. The next morning, the rays of the rising sun, framed by a sky of azure blue, shined brightly through their bedroom window, landing on my face. What a pretty morning! It's often said each day brings its own gift. Lying warm as toast, between my still sleeping grandparents, looking out at the beautiful sky, I was wondering what else I might get for Christmas? That pleasant thought lasted for about two seconds, when the full realization and guilt of my bad deed the day before, hit me like a ton of bricks. I was in deep trouble and I was going to get a whipping, with a switch, I had to cut off a tree myself, on Christmas day. My cousins were coming, and all would know I killed Papaw and Granny's red rooster Lollipop.

Lying quietly between my sleeping grandparents, I began thinking of how to tell them about my killing Lollipop, and how sorry I was. There was no easy way. Guilt is a hard thing to explain away. No one would understand nor sympathize. I couldn't blame them. I had been wrong playing with my BB gun like that, and I was truly sorry.

Then, as the sun's rays continued bathing their little farmhouse window with sunshine, I heard the "cockle-doodle-doo" greeting, that farm roosters give the sun each morning, all over the world. I must be imagining things. Did Granny and Papaw have another rooster I didn't know anything about? I lay quiet as a mouse, listening attentively. Sure enough, another "cockle-doodle-doo" came loud and clear. Sounded like Lollipop to me! I had to know! Jumping up out of the bed, confusing my grandparents by my sudden exit, I ran to look out the kitchen window. Sure enough, standing on the lip of Papaws buckboard, from where I had rested my gun and was shooting him in the rear end yesterday, perched a very much alive, Lollipop, greeting the morning sun.

Oh, my lord, how relieved! I was never so glad to see a mean chicken in my life! Apparently, the BB had knocked him out for a good long time but hadn't killed him. He had recovered just in time to greet the morning sun, giving me a Christmas Miracle! Oh thank you Jesus! Thank you, Lollipop! What a different Christmas Day this will be!

179

Benn Wasson

Dear reader, I've kept this story to myself all these years, until now! You're the first one I've told. Almost!

TWO RED PENCILS

There are two memories of gift incidents in my early childhood, which have never left me! One was the banana cookie on my sixth birthday. The other, I will now reveal.

It was Christmas Day, at Granny and Papaw Benn's house. That morning I had received a miraculous gift of Christmas beyond my dreams. My unintended shot yesterday to the head of old Lollipop had not proved fatal. I would not get a Christmas Day whipping where I would have to go outside and cut my own switch.

Papaw and Granny had a horse, one cow, one hog, several hens, and of course the cantankerous rooster named Lollipop. The one I had shot in the head. There was a vegetable garden next to the barn, the big peach tree, a small field of corn, and Papaws hunting, fishing, and fur trapping skills, which was considerable, kept them reasonably fed. He could set a mink set with the best of them.

I watched him set one once. He had a small spade and dug a round hole in the side of the creek bank at waters edge. Smoothed out the sides so to make it appear like a muskrat or another mink might be using it on a regular basis. He would then set a steel trap at the entrance, hoping to catch a mink traveling through who might be checking out what was in the hole. Before he left the set, he pulled out a small jar of smelly fish bait that was "good and ripe" and sprinkled it around the hole. Mink love fish! You could smell the content from the jar a city block away.

It had been a dry year. The small creeks, frequented by mink searching for food or a mate, had dried up. Mink hides brought the most money of any fur on the market by a considerable margin. Maybe up to thirty dollars a pelt! Papaw had not caught a single mink this year. Money was even more scarce than usual. Several of my cousins were there. Vegetables from the garden, pork meat from the hog they had raised and butchered just before Christmas, provided us with a fine Christmas dinner. Again, one of Granny's terrific peach cobblers, thanks to the Alberta peach tree, served with whipped cream, compliments of their milk cow, left us contented and happy.

Presents were to be handed out after dessert. When it was time to hand out the presents, Granny, with a pained look on her face, which I will never forget, gathered the children around.

"Papaw didn't catch any mink this year children so we can't afford to give you as much as we would like. However, love is more important in life than presents, and we want you to know how much we love each and every one of you. All I was able to purchase for each of you this Christmas are two red pencils. What can you do with just a pencil? Why with a pencil you can learn to write! Writing is one of the most important things in this life you can learn. Learning to write means you can learn to spell, do arithmetic problems, make up a poem, write a note on valentine's day to your sweetheart, help you become successful in life, and maybe someday, even become rich!"

She went on to tell us, "The color of the blood of God's son, Jesus Christ, who died for our sins, was red. Our country is now at war and the red blood of our boys and men, right here from our own neighborhood, is being shed to protect the life of everyone here. Red is one of the colors of our American flag. Red is the color of fire that keeps us warm on cold days and winter nights. Finally, the good things we bring to the table, like apples and strawberries are red, and red is the color of the leaves on our trees that provide us with such beauty in the fall!"

"So, when walking up to the front of your classroom to sharpen these pencils, remember all the things that touch your life which are red, and you just might recall that these two red pencils are one of the Christmas presents you will remember most of all."

I still remember, Granny! Thank you!

BUT FOR THE GRACE OF GOD!

It had been a couple months since the episode of the cattle stampede! It was so frightening we never talked about it much. I never told a soul that I got halfway across the barbed wire fence and was so scared I couldn't lift my left leg. Not even Stanley.

It was hot, just after the Fourth of July picnic. The fourth was a big occasion in our little town of just five hundred and seventy-seven. There wasn't enough money to hire a band. However, loving music himself and being an enterprising fellow, our mayor had planned for prisoners from the state penitentiary to come and play music for us. They played terrific! All were dressed in white uniforms so they could easily be spotted if they tried to run away. Two guards with shotguns always stood on each side of the bandstand.

The music was great! The grownups assembled a floor of parquet wood in front of the bandstand, so townspeople could dance to the music. Mom had taught me how to dance a step or two at home listening to the radio. "Take two steps forward and one back and try and keep in time to the music." I caught on fast!

My Dad had been drafted in the army, along with several other young men in our little town. The band played a slow song and to my horror my Mom said, "Get up, we're going to dance to this one!"

"No! Everybody will make fun of me!"

"Nonsense!"

Then she pulled me out on the dance floor. The trumpet player took the lead and stepped out in front of the other band members and played a song called Stardust! Beautiful song! Two steps forward and one back! After we sat back down, she smilingly said, "Now that wasn't that hard was it?"

I must admit, the music was wonderful, and I saw one of the girls in my class smile at me rather admiringly as I danced by. My heart indeed skipped a beat and I stole another look at her the next time Mom and I danced by again. I was the only boy my age that got on the dance floor!

I sat the rest of the evening listening to the band. They were wonderful! I guess if you're sitting in prison all day with nothing to do, you get to practice a lot. The grown-ups were quite respectful and took the prisoners sandwiches, tea, and cake. Whenever one of them had to go to the toilet, a guard would walk them there and back.

There was one old woman in town that came to every dance. Grown ups said she was mentally imbalanced. I think there must be one in every town. She always wore the same thing. A black dress, black stockings, black shoes, and a black hat with a yellow plastic rose pinned on the left side. No one would dance with her of course, since she was mentally imbalanced. She loved to dance and solved that problem by putting her hands on her hips and commenced dancing all around the floor all by herself. It was kind of jig, dance step. They said when she was young, she fell in love with a young man from Texas. The week before they were to marry, he went back to Texas and left her an "I'm sorry" note and a dozen yellow roses on her doorstep. People think that's what made her go off the range.

Whenever you'd see her, she'd be wearing that black hat, with the plastic yellow rose pinned on the side. Wore it every day. When asked why she always wore the rose, she would look ever so sad and say, "It is to remind me that my sweetheart has left me and gone back to Texas. People in Texas liked yellow roses." Then she would add, "He'll only be gone for a little while, and will be coming back for me any day now."

Knowing the story, I felt sad for her as she paused, all alone, in the middle of the dance floor waiting for the next song. As soon as the band started playing, she would put her hands on her hips, and doing that little jig step, dance away back to the imaginary world, where she would remain the rest of her life.

I was sitting on the bandstand step, just a few feet away from where the prisoners were playing when Stanley came up and sat down beside me.

"Hot ain't it!"

"Yeah but the music's good!"

"I hear the fish are biting down on Salt River! Catching big flatheads! Some up to thirty-five pounds or better!"

Wow! Flathead catfish are a prize. They taste better than other catfish. More like a walleyed pike. Nothing on the planet is better than fried catfish, especially flatheads.

"My Mom would sure know what to do with a big flathead catfish like that," I said. "By ourselves?"

"Sure! We got along all right out at Lick Crick didn't we!

"Uh huh!" I was thinking about the bawling cattle and my unresponsive left leg that had suddenly became petrified while sitting astraddle the barbed wire fence.

"I've already talked to my Dad. He said he would take us down there, fish awhile with us himself, and then head on home and pick us up the next morning."

The possibility of another adventure was beginning to trigger my imagination. Ten-year-old kids, pulling a giant flathead catfish out of Salt River, would be an enhancing reminder to the townsfolk that the two mighty adventurers had returned, victorious once again! Hurrying off home I shouted back "I'll go ask Mom! Talk to you in the morning!"

She was frying a pork chop, when I walked in. Smelled great!

"Mom can I go fishing with Stanley out to Salt River and stay all night?"

"Twenty-five miles is an awful way off! Something bad could happen out there and we couldn't get to you very fast if it did."

Since neither Stanley nor I had thought it prudent to tell our mothers about the possibility of our being trampled to death by the cattle stampede, I followed Stanley's lead line of reasoning.

"Everything turned out hunky dory out there at Lick Creek didn't it?" (Hale Mary full of grace under my breath).

"Who's taking you out there?"

"Stanley's, Dad. He's going to fish awhile with us, then come back for us the next morning."

"Well if he's going to stay with you awhile and see that everything's o.k. I suppose you can go."

"Thanks Mom!" I said giving her a big hug. "Can I have some money tomorrow for fishing line and hooks?"

"The government don't send us much from your Dad being in the army, but I guess I've got enough for that."

187

She unfolded a dollar bill and counted out six quarters.

"It would be nice if you brought us back a nice big catfish!"

"I'll try Mom!"

In those days, the government sent most of the meat, cheese and butter off to the fighting men in the war. Dried beans in the stores were readily available. Protein and meat of any kind was mighty scarce, and not routinely seen in grocery stores.

The next morning, I went down to Stanley's Dad's store to see where he was.

"He's finishing up mowing Miss Seller's yard," said his Dad, whose name was Gilbert.

Stanley got seventy-five cents for mowing her yard, which in those days was the equivalent of fifteen candy bars.

"You can sweep the floor while you're waiting. Looks like I've got three more broken oatmeal cookies! I'll take you boys fishing right after noon."

Gilbert, and I had worked out an arrangement. I loved oatmeal cookies. Still do! In those days, they did not sell cookies in bags or cardboard boxes. Cookies came in a big wooden box. The tops were open so customers would reach into the wooden box and pick out however many cookies they wanted and put them in a brown paper sack. Often as not, they would break a cookie or two while reaching into the box. Gilbert couldn't sell broken cookies! Whenever Stanley was out mowing someone's yard, Gilbert, knowing my fondness for oatmeal cookies, would offer me all the broken cookies if I would sweep the floor. Oatmeal cookies sold for five cents apiece. Broken cookie halves tasted just as good as whole ones. We made a deal!

I must say a word or two more about Stanley's Dad, Gilbert, lest I forget, as he should not be forgotten!

THE HUMMING GHOST

Gilbert was a tall, lanky, thoughtful man, who ran a local grocery store. Loved to fish and hunt. He had a bit of college, could converse with you on many topics, including astrology. One day while in the store waiting on Stanley, he said, "How many stars do you think there are in the big dipper?"

I had looked at the stars many times and marveled that two of them, sure enough, formed the image of a dipper.

"I don't rightly know" I replied.

"'There's seven."

"Didn't know that!"

"How many do think there are in the little dipper?"

"Can't say I know that either. Five I'd guess."

"Seven! They both have the exact same number of stars. If your schoolteacher asks that in class, you'll probably be the only one who knows the answer."

Like I said, he had been to college.

Gilbert was also a crack shot! He had the best shotgun in town. A double-barreled, L.C. Smith that would hit whatever you pointed it at. The opening day of quail season always fell on November 10th. Everyone in town loved the delicacy of fried quail. Some said it was better than chicken! Served along with hot biscuits, cream gravy, and mashed potatoes, it made a meal any housewife was proud to serve. And any man, boy, or girl, delighted in eating it!

On November 10th in Missouri, every able-bodied man and bigger kids stopped work or played hooky and went quail hunting. Today was no exception. It was late afternoon, and Gilbert hadn't yet had the chance to go.

He closed the store early, put on his hunting coat, broke open a box of shells, number eight shot, and started walking towards the western edge of town where he knew quail was plentiful. Right away a covey got up in front of him. He shot twice, and two quails were quickly put into his hunting coat. He kept an eye on the coveys' flight and noted where they landed. He carefully walked to that spot. Birds raised again, he shot twice more, and put two more plump quails in his hunting coat. Like I said, Gilbert was a crack shot! One more would make a fine meal for the family and he noticed the remaining covey landed next to the town cemetery. The sun was close to setting, so he walked quickly in that direction, as only minutes of shooting time was left.

He could hear the quail calling each other, trying to regroup for the night. Sounded like one was right next to the cemetery fence. Light was fading fast. Easing closer to the spot where he thought the quail might have landed, he readied his gun for a possible shot. In the twilight, the mind can play tricks on a person, imagine things are there, that are not. When he glanced over at the cemetery, he suddenly saw a white object floating over a tombstone, then it went back down. "By thunder" he thought, "am I seeing things or am I seeing a ghost!" Straining his eyes in the dimming light, the white object floated up over the tombstone again, went back down then rose back up again. His hair was starting to stand up on the back of his neck! This was a cemetery, and sure enough he was seeing a ghost!

He had never heard how one should confront a ghost. If something was not of this world, and scared the pants off you, maybe you ought to defend yourself and shoot it. What if you didn't shoot it, and it took off after him? Self-preservation is life's first priority. With shaking hands, he slipped off the guns safety and slowly raised the double-barreled L.C. Smith.

The ghost went down again to the grave by the tombstone, he was hoping it had left for good, but then it came back up again, and then quickly went back down again. The ghost's body must be buried there! Maybe they come out at night! Gilbert decided the next time it came up he was going to shoot! Then he thought he heard a sound. He paused to pull on the trigger. He did hear something! It was faint humming like that of a woman's voice, humming a melody of some kind. Maybe that was the woman who was buried there, and her ghost had risen and was humming a song she liked. This was getting edgy! Maybe she came out at night and grabbed anybody she could find and took them back down to the grave with her. The white ghost rose again, and Gilbert, looking into the depths of the unknown, took dead aim, figuring whatever he was seeing must be bad, then resumed a slow squeeze on the trigger. In the fading light, it seemed like he could almost make out a facial image. He might be seeing what the lady ghost looked like when she was alive. This was awful! He could hardly control the shaking of his hands. Whatever this apparition was, it surely must present a mortal danger to his life!

He strengthened his pull on the trigger. As scary as this thing was, he would shoot both barrels at once. That for sure ought to knock it to kingdom come! Steadying his shaking arm for an accurate shot, the hair on his head stood straight up when a voice said, "You're quail hunting kind of late aren't you Gilbert?"

With that his knees buckled, he dropped the L.C. Smith to the ground and grabbed hold of the cemetery fence to keep from falling.

"Oh my god, oh my god, the ghost is coming right towards me and it knows my name. Might be coming to take me right on down to the fires of hell for even thinking about shooting in a cemetery!"

Then a woman's face appeared right in front of him, humming the melody he had heard. Good lord! It's wearing a bonnet! Wearing a white bonnet! It looked like the face of Mrs. Abigail Hawkins! That is her face, but she's not dead, she's still alive!

"Mind if I walk back to town with you Gilbert?"

He was confused!

"Why no Mrs. Abigail," trying to compose himself, "be mighty glad to have some company."

"I've been down here tidying up Jim's grave before the winter storms come," she said. "Takes a lot of bending up and down, and my back hurts a good bit!"

That was it! He hadn't seen a ghost at all. It was Mrs. Abigail's white bonnet he saw raising up and down while tidying up her husband's grave. He'd almost shot her!

"Shoot anything?" she asked.

Picking up the L.C. Smith from the ground and putting it back on safety, he turned his head, looked at her, swallowed hard and said "Four quail! Was hoping to get one more for the table," he choked out!

"There's always tomorrow," she said.

He turned his head looking at her again, thinking, you can thank the merciful lord for that Miss Abigail!

While in church the following Sunday, Gilbert decided right then and there that decisions, made in haste, or fear, or anger, need to be slowed down a little, as they can alter one's life forever, maybe eternity. He measured his thoughts, answers, and actions more slowly thereafter. Like I said, Stanley's Dad was a thoughtful good man! And never again hunted around a graveyard.

TWO HOUR SHIFTS

It was two in the afternoon when Stanley came in from mowing Mrs. Seller's yard and said, "Are we ready?"

"Pretty much so," I replied. "I dug some fishing worms from behind the barn this morning. Mom gave me a blanket, money to buy fishing lines and hooks. If your Dad will give us some bacon and eggs and that old iron skillet, we'll be good to go!"

He quickly gathered up the supplies plus six sodas and a jug of water and pronounced, "It's time to go!"

When you're young, and full of anticipation for adventure, not much thought is put into it. You just want to go!

We put our supplies, bait, and sleeping blankets in the back of the pickup. Placed a toolbox over the blankets so they wouldn't blow out and jumped into the front seat with Stanley's Dad. On the way he asked if we had a flashlight.

"I put four batteries in," Stanley said! Checked out the batteries too! They're good!"

Riding along Gilbert said "Looks like it's going to be a clear night. Should be able to see the stars good tonight, might even be able to see both the big and little dipper." I remembered they each had seven stars.

In about twenty minutes we reached Salt River.

"Pretty big river boys! Pretty deep too! Sure you're up to staying here all night by yourselves?"

"Sure, we are!" I piped up.

Stanley added in his affirmation! The silver bridge stretching over the river was a formidable structure, nearly a quarter mile long. Tall enough that riverboats and barges could go underneath without hitting the lower steel beams, that is if the river was not running high.

We eagerly jumped out of the truck, grabbed our gear and were ready for our big night out.

"See you boys about nine in the morning!"

"Ok Dad," said Stanley as the pickup kicked up a small cloud of road dust on the service road just before getting onto the pavement. Always a little bit of that lonesome feeling sets in when watching your lifeline to safety fade away in the distance. Stanley cleared his throat, "Guess we better set our lines!"

"Suppose so," I said and began unwinding the white cotton fishing line I had bought at the hardware store.

I cut a few willow poles with my dad's hatchet, then noticed under the bridge close to where we would be camping, piles of logs and brush that had been lodged there by high water. Climbing out there would be risky, but deep water is the perfect spot where a big flathead catfish might hang out. I cut me a short pole, tied on the line, got out my biggest fishing hook, loaded it with worms, and stuck a tiny crawdad on the very tip of the hook. There was no dirt out on the log pile, so I lodged the pole between two small logs, so if I did catch something, it wouldn't pull it away.

With lines set, we found some rocks, placed them in a circle, gathered firewood to put in the middle, lit a fire, and cooked the usual bacon and eggs.

It was a clear night. The myriad of stars was breathtaking to look at. Right away I found the big dipper, and with a little more looking, found the little dipper as well. Seven stars were in each.

We dropped off to sleep to be awakened by the buzzing of swarms of mosquito's, biting us at will. We tried to cover up with our blankets to no avail. Then Stanley said, "Let's go up on the bridge, maybe they won't be up that high!"

Sure enough, when we got out on the pavement, walked to the middle of the bridge, not a mosquito could be found. What a moment of bliss! We stood there enjoying our freedom from the mosquito persecution for a moment, when a car's headlights came into view and we edged over to the rail so it wouldn't hit us. It soon passed, and we continued to marvel how nice it was up there. Soon headlights appeared again, and we went back to the rail. It was a cattle hauler. We recognized the smell as it drove by. While we were leaning against the bridge rail, two more pickups came through.

Stanley said, "Wonder how deep the water is down there?"

"I've heard it's twenty feet or more," I replied.

Then I had that uncomfortable feeling that fear brings on...I couldn't swim! If cars or trucks didn't see us, and wavered over close to the rail, and I jumped, it would be certain death. If they hit us, it could possibly be the same outcome or be crippled for life.

"Stanley, do you think it's safe to stay up here with cars and trucks coming through?"

"Oh, we'll be all right, we can see them coming for a half mile away."

197

"I suppose so," I replied, glancing at the rail with uncertainty, realizing that he could swim, and I couldn't!

A plan was made to gain a little rest while escaping the mosquitoes. We would sleep in the middle of the bridge one would stay awake and keep watch, while the other slept. If a car or truck came from the north, we'd sound the alarm, grab our blankets, and go to the east rail. If it came from the south, we would get up and go to the west rail. Seemed logical. Stanley said he would stay awake and keep watch the first two hours, then it would be my turn and I would keep watch for two hours and so on until daybreak.

I laid my blanket down and was just drifting off to sleep when Stanley nudged me and said "Wake up! There's a car coming from the south!"

I grabbed my blanket and headed for the east rail. It went speeding by at a high speed. Looked like teenage boys driving and drinking something or the other out of a bottle. It probably wasn't soda pop.

I had only napped for an hour, so I lay back down again on my blanket and promptly went back to sleep. It seemed like it wasn't five minutes before I felt a nudge from Stanley again and heard him saying, "Your two hours are up!"

I said, "O.K.," stood up and walked around a few feet from Stanley who had already lain down and fallen fast to sleep.

I could hear an owl hooting off in the distance. Sound travels a long way over water. Bullfrogs were croaking away at a frenzied pitch, and the sound of mosquito's buzzing below was a grim reminder that it would be punishment, to try and sleep down below by the water.

A full moon came up, providing enough light to walk around on the bridge and see the centerline of the bridge's highway. I looked up in the sky and saw the big dipper again but couldn't find the little one.

No cars had come through since the teenage boys whizzed by. A whippoorwill started calling from a sycamore tree not far from where we were sleeping. Since we were up so high, we were not far from his perch in the tree. Almost like a special bridge side performance. I always found the nostalgic and mournful sound of whippoorwills fascinating.

Stanley had lent me his watch. I picked up the flashlight to see the time and saw that I had an hour to go. I was really tired, and it occurred to me that if I lay down for just a moment or two, rested, say no more than five minutes or so, I could then get up, walk around a little more, and easily stay awake until my two hours was up.

I laid down on my blanket, put my hands behind my head to serve as a pillow, and wondered if we might be catching a fish below on the lines we had set. No cars were coming. I looked up at the stars and found the big dipper again. Sure enough, the seven stars were still there. Straining my eyes harder, I found the little dipper. Yep, seven stars were there just like Gilbert had said. On a clear night, stars are simply beautiful. Millions of different worlds must be up there. Wonder if anybody like us lives in those worlds? I was so tired; I thought it wouldn't hurt if I closed my eyes for just a minute or two. As the cloak of sleep closed over my boyish eyes, I dreamed a spaceship landed right beside Stanley and me. A door opened and a man with a shiny silver suit stepped out and said "Wake up! Want to take a ride?"

"Where 's to?"

"The Orion."

"Where's that?"

"You've been looking at it all night!" he replied.

Then someone was shaking me, and I heard the words "Wake up" again. Sunlight filled my sleep and I saw Stanley standing there shaking my left shoulder and saying, "Wake up! You went to sleep, and we've been laying out here half the night, right in the middle of the bridge, and could have been run over and killed!" We then heard a truck coming and we decided to get off the bridge in a hurry!

Quickly grabbing our blankets, we ran down below! The mosquitoes were gone! Thank goodness!

"I'm sorry Stanley," I said.

"We were lucky you know!"

Then, as sometimes happens when one has dodged a bullet, he laughed, looked at me and said, "Man, were we ever lucky!" We lit a fire under the iron skillet and fried up some bacon and eggs. And yes, we were very lucky that night!

Stanley's dad rolled up a few moments later.

"You boys have any luck?"

I had caught a ten-pound flathead on the line I had set in the deep water under the bridge. "Yes sir, we did! We had some real good luck."

Stanley gave me a knowing look and said, "Yes dad, we had some really good luck! Outstanding even!" and…of course we had!

FORWARD STEP: A NEARLY PERFECT DAY

Every little girl should have a near perfect day. This was one in the life of my great granddaughter Madison Lee! Praise God she will enjoy many more!

I enjoyed picking her up from school and taking her to nice restaurants for dinner. Today, I had taken her to a fine Italian restaurant, tablecloths, nice waiters, pleasant atmosphere and full upscale cordiality. Upon entering the establishment, my seven-year-old great granddaughter, dressed in a t-shirt and jeans informed me she was underdressed! Pretty sophisticated thought for age seven. After reminding her she was the prettiest little girl in the place, which she was, attention was turned to savory fragrances coming out of the kitchen, and delicious looking servings being placed on nearby tables. We sat down and had a lovely meal. Three different breads were served. One of the breads was formed in crispy triangles, along with unsalted triangles of butter. Different, and delicious!

Loving her more than my next breath, and always trying to think of something to brighten her little world, my wife and I, the following week, asked her mother if she could spend the weekend with us. She came out to the car wearing a little green and black dress, the one we had bought her some while back and small black shiny shoes with super tiny heels. She said she would like to go to a nice place to have dinner, which is why she said she had worn her nice dress up clothes. Remembering her last experience, it was a given she meant the nice Italian place where we had gone recently.

Carrying her little suitcase, and wearing the dress and shiny shoes, we walked to the car and lo and behold, there was a large rock sticking out of the right rear tire. Hurriedly we drove to Costco before the Run Flat tires exceeded their fifty-mile limit. Made it! Then waited three hours, way past dinnertime, dining on nothing but Costco hot dogs, before we could get a new tire.

Some two months later, June 24th we picked up Madison Lee on a Saturday for an overnight stay. On the way out of the driveway, out of the blue, the indicator light came on, signifying we had a problem with the left front tire. We just couldn't believe this was happening again. We hurried to the nearby Beemer dealership where Madison proceeded to eat an entire bagel with cream cheese the minute we had arrived, while we sat in their waiting area. She was hungry! Luckily, turned out it was a weather change tire pressure problem, nothing serious.

That night, we went to a Mexican food restaurant, dined, and went home to watch a movie. I told my usual nighttime stories. Normally three are expected! On this night, one new one I made up on the spot came out well and got her to laughing.

The morning of the 25th, everyone overslept until nine, even eleven o'clock mass was out. We played pitch and catch for dexterity purposes. Neither eighty-year-old nor seven did too well. Her mother was unsure when she would pick her up, so it was at the last minute that we decided we would make the four o'clock mass. Last one of the week. The four o'clock mass is sometimes called the sinner's mass, being the amount of time party goers, who had been reveling the night before, need to gain a clear head and make it to church.

Our young priest, Father Johnathan, had been Madison's priest at Little Lambs since she was three years old. Now four years later; he was leaving to be a priest for the young college students at the prestigious St. Francis University. She went up to see him as he was greeting incoming churchgoers. They bumped fists and did high fives as a form of greeting, also knowing they were saying goodbye.

Betty had bought her a new pink dress, matching bow for her hair and white shoes with little spikes. Elderly ladies stepped up and told her how pretty she was. And was she ever! Then they asked us to present the daily offering to the priest. The church had three priests, but this day we presented the offering to none other than, Father Jonathan, his last mass ever to be held at Good Shepherd Church. Madison carried the sacramental host (body of Christ), Betty and I carried the wine. Father Johnathan bowed to us as Madison beamed and handed him the hosts. We three bowed in return. A perfect moment for her with the first priest she had ever known.

On the way down the aisle, after mass was concluded, Madison and Father Johnathan again made eye contact and he reached over towards her and they bumped fists on his last trip down Good Shepherds aisle. When we were departing and leaving out the door, Father Johnathan greeted all who had come, and he and Madison did one final high five. Silent tears flowed down her cheeks after high fiving Father Jonathan for the last time. As he walked away, she sensed that part of her childhood was walking away with him. He was a good man and a good Priest, and Madison of course, one of earth's special treasures.

Being appropriately dressed, wearing her nice clothes, we left church and went to the fine Italian restaurant we all loved, for a delicious dinner. We took pictures for keepsakes, to remember the time when Madison Lee enjoyed a near perfect day. Thank you, God!

Madison, Betty and Me

POSTSCRIPT

It had been decades since I had last seen Stanley. When I asked the few people left from our little town of his whereabouts, no one knew, or whether he was still alive. Then, someone came up with a phone number. I found him! My wife and I drove to his home in southern Missouri. He lived on a hill. Instead of us having to ask which house was which, Stanley was standing out front on his doorstep, waiting for us to arrive. His hair had turned to silver, as had mine. Both had stayed married to the same sweethearts of our youth – and both were blessed with children – and grandchildren, and great grandchildren and had reared wonderful families.

There's a unique thing about childhood friends. In five minutes of conversation, time reversed itself, and it was back to "Stanley and Me" again, talking and acting as if we had seen each other just yesterday morning.

They say memories of the heart never forget. I like that saying. Memories of Stanley, Jimmie, Gilbert, my Mom, Dad, and Frisky from the little town we grew up in, will forever remain in my heart!

TAILGATE

"Footsteps Through My Mind"

I had sent the recording studio in Nashville a tape of the song I'd written. To my surprise, they liked it! They called and said, "Come on in, we'll record in two weeks. If the session comes out good, we'll release it as a single." Wow! Our band, "The Hard Times," from Ralls County's tiny town of Center, Missouri, was to go to Nashville and record in two weeks. This was heady stuff! Everybody knows everybody else in a tiny town like Center. People who live in small places like that care for each other. I miss it to this day.

As a small boy, I used to eat hamburgers in guitarist Carlon's grandmother's tiny restaurant for fifteen cents apiece. Lead guitar Swony's uncle had been married to my aunt. Before that my aunt had dated Carlon's Dad. His Dad played the fiddle. Drummer Bob's daughter, Nyla, sang background with my sister, Peggy, and her friend Lana. David, bass player, was Bob's brother, Nyla's uncle. Later, Swony married my sister Peggy, and Lana married David. Like I said, everybody knows everybody else in little towns like Center or they are related. Confusing? Little intertwined towns often are!

The studio had called in two Nashville pros to come in and help out on the session. The hall of famed steel guitarist, Weldon Myrick, and one high range lady soprano singer. When the countdown came, and the music started, the moment was so emotional I choked up and had to start it over again. When the record was released, radio personality Joe Lewis, from the small country station KPCR, in Bowling Green, Missouri, liked the song and started playing it right away. Joe was the first one in the nation to play it. Then much to my surprise, Chris Lane started playing it on WIL, the big country station in St. Louis! Went up to the top ten! That's a big market! Then Don Rhea of the big country station KCKN in Kansas City started playing it. Went up to ten there as well. Another big market! Then juke boxes started playing it all over the country. New York stations were playing it and Santa Barbara played it heavily for the longest time. I couldn't imagine people out there in their million-dollar California houses calling in to hear "Footsteps". Beethoven maybe, surely not someone from Center!

My Dad heard it for the first time on a juke box. He cashed a dollar bill for some change, got a chair and sat down right in front of the juke box so he could hear it good and played it four times. He got up and said, "Bennie wrote that for his mother!" You were right Dad!

Who would think folks from a tiny little place like Center could do a thing like that? Write and record a little song that played throughout the nation and decades later is still being streamed globally! Well we did, and someday I later might get the chance to tell you more about it. I hope you enjoyed the read! May peace and joy walk with you always!

"SEE WHEN YOU LOOK…FEEL WHEN YOU TOUCH…AND REMEMBER!"

~Bennie Wasson

A bientôt!

About Benn Wasson

Upon graduating from high school at an early age, Benn Wasson, was invited to leave home by his stepfather, and make his own way through life at the age of sixteen. Landing a job at A & P Grocery in Hannibal, Missouri, and renting a bedroom at the YMCA for ten dollars a week, he would often sit on the park bench down by the bank of the Mississippi River, and wonder where the streams of life would take him.

The answer was...quite a far piece!

First, becoming a sailor on the aircraft carrier U.S.S. Intrepid, which took him to many foreign ports throughout the world. Blessed in the Vatican audience by Pope Pius XII. Being a nondrinker and nonsmoker, he used funds left from his meager sailors' pay wisely to visit the many historical sights of Europe. Went to the Louvre Museum in Paris to view the Mona Lisa, visited the marketplaces in Istanbul, spent a moonlight night sitting atop a column of one of the lion cages in the middle of the Roman Coliseum.

Second, worked his way through college becoming the first in the history of his family to obtain a college degree.

Third, became a businessman, member of the agricultural press covering the United States from coast to coast.

Fourth, followed his passion for music by becoming a singer, songwriter, and recording artist.

On later trips to Rome, was blessed to be in the private audiences twice, by Pope John Paul II. Now Saint John Paul II.

Lastly, introduces his first novel/autobiography "Footsteps Through My Mind."

Wonder what will come next?

DISCOGRAPHY

RECORDINGS OF BEN WASSON COMPOSITIONS

Classic Sweet Country - CD/Album

- Lonely Much Too Long
- Goodbye Sunshine
- First Thing in the Morning
- Everyday Kind of Man
- I'll Be Going Where I Please
- Everybody's Some King of A Fool
- Macoupin Station Train
- Room #333
- A Cold Day In Dallas
- When Love's Gone Away
- God Bless Ya' Brother
- Footsteps Through My Mind
- Wait For Me Virginia
- I Still Remember Loving You

Ode To Baby Boomers - CD/ALBUM

- Ode to Baby Boomers
- Winds of Change

Sweet Rockabilly Blues - CD/ALBUM

- Papillon

TRANSITIONS - CD/ALBUM

- Just Another Misty Night (in Southern Carolina)
- Lady's Choice
- Late Sweet Night Memories
- Adios C'Est La Vie
- Long Haired Midnite Woman
- Powder Blue
Available: https://store.cdbaby.com/Artist/BenWasson

Recorded at Norm Petty Studio

- Am I Still Your Number One
- Fool Again
- Little Wallflower
- Jada Boom
- It's Springtime Baby
- Bellavina

See: http://norvajakmusic.com/

Made in the USA
Las Vegas, NV
27 October 2021